The Difference

a memoir

S.A Blair

For my dad, and the promise I made him.

Names have been omitted and some details have been left out to protect the identity and integrity of those involved.

Prelude

I locked my gaze with a loose carpet thread on the floor and I imagined myself pulling on it until the whole world came unraveled. My thoughts raced in circles around a room that felt as though it were shrinking, losing air somehow, as I searched for the words to describe to this woman how I was feeling.

How was I feeling?

A vast array of emotions bubbled just below the surface of my skin, threatening to boil over at a moment's notice. The feelings that I was experiencing that I seemed to be lacking the words to articulate whirled around so rapidly it felt as though my breath could barely maintain pace with the dips and dives of the rollercoaster that I had suddenly found myself on.

I didn't ask to be here.

I searched the inventory of words within myself to try and answer this question-how are you feeling?
A hint of relief, maybe? Like the wind had been knocked out of me as the illusion of normalcy I had maintained over the years was swept away.

Reeling myself in from my drifting thoughts; I was reminded that I wasn't alone in the room, and I lifted my attention from the patterns on the floor to my therapist who was seated in front of me.
She looked upon me with the sort of patient understanding that made me feel at ease. She had kind eyes, deeply considerate pools of brown set just behind a pair of black, wire-rimmed glasses.
Her shoulder length brown hair was thick and wavy, coming to rest on either side of her calmly expressive face.

I felt considerably removed from my body; the words she spoke sounded soft and muffled as she explained to me that the rehab that I was in had one of the best trauma therapy programs in the country.

"How would you feel about trying EMDR?"

she asked me, perfectly still aside from the repetitive motion of tracing the tip of her pen with her finger.

I nodded my head slowly, returning my eyes to the floor as I mulled it over; I was certainly willing to try anything if it would help me feel better.
Any resistance towards suggestion had been beaten out of me over the years of my addiction and persistent efforts towards self-destruction.
As we finished the rest of the session, she gave me a final "welfare check," to make sure that I would be okay sitting with my thoughts for the rest of the day.

"I will be safe."

I promised her.

I left her office in a daze, attempting to process what all of this meant.

I, with the help of the rest of the world, convinced myself that I was crazy, that there was no reason behind my erratic, out of control behavior. I adopted the version of me that the world had offered me-that I was a bad person-rather than a sick person who needed help and healing. Neither I nor the world ever knew any better, I guess.

Thick, hot tears were rising as I made my way outside to go for a walk on the trail.

The rehab I was in was a beautiful facility tucked neatly away in a small town in the mountains. For the first time in my life, I had begun to find some semblance of peace there.

I kept my head down and my eyes lowered to the few feet of ground that lay directly in front of me as I rushed through the building, desperate to get outside where I felt that perhaps I could breathe again.

If people were looking at or speaking to me, I could not hear or see them. I placed one foot in front of the other and I continued to move forward-no matter what.

Swinging the large wooden doors open, I was hit with the crisp, cool air washing over my face. The world around me was a symphony of my staggered breathing,

birds chirping, and the gravel crunching beneath my feet.
I felt as though something other than myself was operating my body like a machine, moving my limbs, and driving me forward, when inside, I was crumbling.

I glanced back to make sure that no one was watching, I turned off the trail and disappeared into the trees, making my way to my usual quiet spot.
Taking my place on the ground beneath a towering, beautiful, old Cottonwood tree, I had never felt more raw, present, and aware than I was in that moment.
The sun was just settling down over the mountain and I admired the way it cast its golden light between the branches, setting the tips of the tall, mountain prairie grass aglow.

Taking long, deep breaths to steady the quake within me, I began to crack as I allowed the emotions within me to finally spill over.
As the hot tears streamed down my face, I couldn't help but notice the relief that I felt amidst the greatest pain.

***

Sometimes I hear God in the trees.
I sense the presence of something greater in the way the wind moves the leaves that hang from every branch, softly rustling in the breeze, my hair moves in perfect synchronicity.
Sitting on the porch, I can feel the sun warming the tops of my feet-one crossed over the other, barefoot toes stretching out in the light. As the sunlight warms my skin, I feel it warm my soul and something stirs in me.
I am reminded of myself.
A profound sense of peace washes over me, I hear nothing else, not even my own breath, as everything that I am and everything that is merges in this one moment.

Everything becomes the trees.
Or maybe it always was.

I always loved listening to them as a kid, and that part of me has never faltered or faded away.
As I grow, there are parts of me that are left behind.
Pieces of me that I shed like a skin as a new me is reborn from the flame and the ash.
I have left many wakes of destruction behind me; I have burned many bridges.

Yet there is this deep sense of self that I find when I quiet my thoughts long enough to just listen to the trees. When I am outside, I am whole. I am me.

I remember my life the way that one remembers a dream.

***

1

I used to sing quietly to myself when my parents would fight. Anything to drown out the screaming insults and slamming doors. Tucked beneath the covers on my bed, studying the shadows cast by small lumps of plaster spackled on the ceiling, softly murmuring the words to a song or a nursery rhyme and pretending that I was somewhere else.

I would drift away in the depths of my imagination, and I would remain there, where it was safe, until the house inevitably fell quiet again.

Though his drinking and his rage made a relationship between my dad and I near impossible, I still looked up to him for many things. He was my father, after all. He owned his own construction company, and every now and again he would take me with him to one of his job sites. We would walk along the grounds, as he pointed things out, teaching me about what part of the

building process they were in and all the finer details of the job, none of which I really understood, but I was simply happy to be a part of it.
There was a feeling of importance, riding around with the boss of the whole operation.
I regarded that my father was an intelligent man; I could tell by the blueprints he would map out for each project. There were many nights spent perched on the kitchen counter, struggling to comprehend as he stood across from me, beer in hand, tiny beads of sweat lining his excited face, as he attempted to explain the concepts of other dimensions to me.
Scribbling out these little diagrams, waving his hands around the air enthusiastically as he attempted to paint a picture of the words that he spoke. You could feel his passion from across the room.

He was always troubled, though. His demons and nightmares past were etched in deep creases on his face, casting shadows when they rose to the surface. You could feel his pain just by looking at him, though he would never admit that it was there.
Through the grapevine of our family tree, I sometimes heard stories about his life growing up. The abuse that himself, his siblings, and my grandmother endured. It was one of those family things that everyone kind of knows about and no one ever wants to talk about.
We sweep those things under the rug and tidy up the dirt and dust so that we can continue to smile in the face of today.

It's always there, though…the past.
Lying in wait.

***

A feral child: I sunk the tips of my fingers deep into the soil, feeling the warm breath of the Earth nestled against the soft chill of the air as the sky opened, giving way to a light rain.

I loved the rain.

I would imagine it coming down and washing away all the hurt, making everything new again.

As a kid, I spent as much time as I could outside, wandering throughout the landscape in the front and back of the house. Watching the trees swaying softly in the breeze, gazing up at their soothing magnificence. The wind would rustle their leaves and I would close my eyes, listening to the stories they would tell.

It was calming for me.

I would pretend like I could just float away, just disappear into nothing and into everything all at once. Crouching down amidst the trees and the shrubs, I felt as though I was hidden away in my own private world. The garden served as my safe place, providing me with a refuge from the chaos that resided in my home and in my heart.

From between the thick branches of the shrubbery, I peeked out from within my sanctuary, fancying myself as some sort of woodland creature. For a while I just sat there, suspended in time, staring at the front door of the two-story suburban house as it sat across from me, quiet and still.

The trees and shrubs that encompassed the yard were neatly and methodically pruned. Hedges of lilac, hydrangea bushes and columbine flowers beautifully coloring the yard with scent and sight, baby aspen trees reaching up for the clouds and slowly growing into maturity.

The lilacs were my favorite; their sweet, floral scent would linger in the early summer air, for just so long as the flowers would bloom, a length of time that was always all too brief.

A favorite thing of mine was to pick the columbine blossoms, bite off the tips of the spurs, and savor the sweet nectar inside.

There was a short walkway leading from the driveway to the front door. Juniper bushes and a variety of white, yellow, and pink daisies grew alongside the sidewalk. There were cobwebs that hung in the corners above the doorway, littered with the tiny skeletal remains of the poor souls that were trapped there.

I wondered where the spiders had gone that had once occupied those webs.

Thunder rolled across the darkening sky, comforting and frightening.

I felt a strange sense of satisfaction imagining how my family would feel when they realized I was missing. In my head I played out all the ways in which they would react—the fear, the feelings of loss and guilt, of wishing that things would have turned out differently; maybe they could have done more.

Eyes locked with that looming green door, waiting for movement, waiting for them to come looking for me, I sat.
Waiting for someone, anyone, to feel my absence.

As the rain continued to fall the air steadily grew colder. A low growl escaped the depths of my stomach, deep and hollow, pleading for food.
I shifted my position impatiently; my feet were falling asleep. The longer I sat, the more unforgiving the ground became beneath me. I would have liked to think that I was brave enough and strong enough to stay out there forever.
I visualized how my life would be-living amongst the trees. It was fun to imagine these things, but when faced with the harsh reality of the elements and the lack of food, my resolve quickly dissipated.

The realization crept over me that the time would not come for them to feel my absence, they would simply move on with their lives and I would be nothing more than a vague memory that they would struggle to recall when brought up in conversation.

"Ah, yes, I think I knew a Sarah once..."

No one was looking for me, no one had even noticed that I was gone. I wanted to stay there forever, I wanted to make them feel bad for losing me, but the cold and the hunger eventually overtook my stubborn nature. Clothes beginning to soak through with moisture, heart drenched in disappointment, I retreated from my rebellious post.

Inside the home my family was carrying on with their lives as usual. My mom standing at the kitchen sink, washing the cherry tomatoes she had picked from the garden, my oldest brother sat on the couch-lost in whatever show he happened to be watching, and my other brother was upstairs in his room, doing whatever it was that he did in there.

I regretfully accepted my role as the unseen child, burying whatever feelings I harbored about it. Wordlessly, I walked into the kitchen, and I opened the fridge to find something to satiate my hunger. I was grateful, at least, that I didn't have to forage for my food today.

As my body temperature warmed and my stomach filled, I quickly forgot about what had happened and the resentments that I harbored, as children often do.

What I did not know is that these things were never forgotten, only buried.

***

Growing up, my mother was my hero for many reasons. Intelligent, funny, and ambitious. I found myself in awe of her, filled with admiration at the way her strength always shown through. She was beautiful, her black hair always done up in soft curls, her large hazel eyes were a trait that I was lucky enough to inherit.

A smile that would light up a thousand dark rooms.

She carried this sort of quiet power, as though she held the force of a thunderstorm within her. She could be gentle though, too.

When my brothers and I would get sick she would lay us down to bed, gently scratching our backs with her long, elegant fingers, and quietly singing us to sleep. I never felt safer than I did in those moments.

As a young adult, my mom had worked hard and landed herself a stable career. It seemed like she was always running off on these business trips, and I always thought to myself how exciting and cool that must be, getting to travel like that. I knew that someday, I wanted to travel too.

I craved the experience of seeing the world outside of the tiny town that we lived in.

She spent most of her free time at home on the weekends, out in the garden, planting and tending to every kind of vegetable imaginable and sculpting our yard into a wonderful place.

Her and I were always the same in that way-our love of gardening and spending time outdoors.

One of my favorite things in the world was when I would get to be outside with her, helping her plant the season's harvest.

As the summer season went on and the garden matured, I would sift through the cherry tomatoes, picking the red and ripe ones and popping them in my mouth, hunting for the ladybugs and the fat green caterpillars that would sometimes terrorize the tomato plants.

I always carried with me this nagging sense that the town that I lived in was much too small for me, and that I was meant for bigger things and, someday, I would show the world just of what I was capable. Maybe it was intuition, or maybe it was just a daydream meant to distract myself from reality.

Not much ever happened in our small town, it was your typical, non-descript, small-town suburbia hidden away in the northern plains of Colorado.

Aside from the abundance of farmland and vast, rolling fields, we had a gas station, a police station, and a dusty

little skatepark where all the teenagers would hang out after school, smoking cigarettes that they snuck from the purses and pockets of their parents.
There was only one stoplight in the whole town, right at the intersection with the white steeple church. If you took a left at that stoplight the road would take you past the elementary and middle schools that sat side by side.

All I ever really had just for myself was the garden, school, and, of course, my imagination.
My family had a few acres of land, and it was there that I would spend most of my free time. Digging up ant hills and examining the larvae within the small tunnels, eating raspberries off the bushes in the garden, and flipping over rocks that lay at the bed of the creek, hunting for crawdad.
Sometimes I would think about sending a message in a bottle down the creek behind our house. I would envision all the places it would go, and who would find and read it, and how many years later it would be.
The neighbors directly to our left had two horses that resided in a barn, and on one of my birthdays they let my friends and I ride them as repayment for the duty our cat conducted for them of killing the barn mice that would startle the horses.

My brothers spent a lot of their free time hanging out with each other and with their friends, and if I wasn't with my best friend, I was usually alone. There was always a sense of separation from my brothers because they were close in age, and both boys, so they related to each other more than they related to me.

I was the youngest, and a girl, so I often felt like an annoyance to them.
I looked up to them and wanted to hang out with them but of course two young boys rarely want their bratty kid sister tagging along, and so I was frequently left behind.

To any outside observer I am certain that our life and our family probably looked ideal. We had the house my father had built for us, the beautiful yard my mother worked tirelessly on, a white cat with big orange spots that was gifted to me on my fourth birthday, and a German Shepard—it was the "American dream." Though, as is the case with many small-town families, we also had our secrets.

Sometimes I wondered if the neighbors could hear my parents screaming at each other at night, if they had any suspicion of who my dad became behind closed doors.
I also wondered if their families were the same way, or if ours was the only one.

***

I adored Christmas.

The twinkling lights, the slow, soulful music, the holiday cheer that seemed to warm the frost-bitten air. It was a time when everyone could pretend.
We would all wrap our smiles with ribbons and bows and for a fleeting period everything seemed okay, everyone seemed happier.
Although I couldn't help but notice the stress that my parents felt regarding money during these times; that was one of the things they fought about the most. So, when holidays came around, and the weight of the responsibility to provide gifts arose, the tension and the fights would escalate in severity and frequency.

My brothers and I had an awful habit of peeping at our presents in the weeks leading up to the big day. We became skilled at it; carefully peeling back the tape so as not to disturb the colorful paper that wrapped and kept secret the surprises underneath.
We simply couldn't wait, we had to know.

On this Christmas, like all the others, I snuck a look at what I was going to get. I eyed every box, picking them up one at a time, deciding which one I wanted to steal a look at.
After carefully surveying each gift, I landed on one of the smaller, square packages.
I held my breath as I gingerly peeled back the tape, reciting one of those fox-hole prayers to not let the wrapping paper tear.

Finally, I got it open, and to my surprise and delight it was a video game that I had been wanting for some time. I was so excited; I just couldn't wait to play it. My parents were supposed to be gone for a while and I figured that gave me just enough time to take the game for a test spin before rewrapping it and placing it back under the tree.
I delicately removed the packaging one piece of tape at a time, and I snuck the game upstairs to the playroom, placing it in the console. My heart fluttered with fear of being caught mixed with giddy excitement.
I played the game for some time and eventually got bored or hungry and turned the gaming console off. Absent-mindedly, I didn't think to take the game out and

put it back where I had snuck it from, and I left it in the PlayStation.

Later that evening, I was tucked away in my room, blissfully unaware of the consequences to come.
My dad burst through the door, shaking with anger,

"You know you're not allowed to look at your presents!"

His voice echoed throughout the room, bouncing off the walls.

My stomach was doing cartwheels when I realized that I had been caught as my eyes fell on the video game CD in his hand. My thoughts raced as I struggled to retrace my steps, wondering how I could have been so stupid as to leave it out.
I was angry at myself for my mistake, and I was terrified of what my father would do.
I began to cry and apologize with sincere regret.
Feeling that I needed a proper punishment, my dad crushed the CD in his hand.
I sincerely felt that my heart had broken into just as many pieces as the game did. I was so angry at my dad for what he had done, but I was even more angry at myself for being stupid enough to get into this mess. If I had only done as I was told, if I had only been patient and waited to open my present, this wouldn't have happened.

"If you can't wait for Christmas like you're told then you don't get your present at all."

He let the broken pieces fall to the floor and the door slammed shut with a harsh finality as he left me. I remained in the center of my bed for some time, tears streaming down my face, my ears burning red hot with anger.

I hated him.

Part of me hoped that maybe he would come back in the room minutes later with sincere remorse over what he had done. He would apologize to me and tell me he loved me and that he was sorry.

My expectations were met by a silent, empty room.

The rest of the holidays went on per usual-minus my present. None of us talked about it, it was as if it never happened, never mattered. It was brushed aside like any other conflict that arose in our household. I gathered up all my hurt feelings and bruised pride in a neat little pile and I kept it all locked away.

***

That night, the house was near silent, aside from the muffled hum of the furnace as it whirred on periodically to keep us warm throughout the night. My brothers were sound asleep, but I sat awake in the dark looking out the window as the shadows stretched by the glow of the streetlights.

My mom was away on one of her frequent business trips and my father who was tasked with the chore of watching us kids was nowhere to be found. It was not the first nor the last time he would come home in the middle of the night.

Often, my brothers and I would stay at my grandma's house. There were many joyful nights spent there, sleeping in my grandma's bed with her while my brothers slept on the couches in the living room. She would make us piping hot Malt O' Meal in the mornings, cooled with a splash of milk and sweetened with sugar. It was such a simple pleasure, but it was one that I always looked forward to whenever we were there. One by one, my dad would pile us all into his truck and haul us over to her house to stay for the weekend. Giddy with excitement, we would happily oblige. I would study my father as he drove, one arm hanging out the window, an open can of Bud Light in the cup holder. He always appeared so calm and cool, yet underneath the shady exterior you could sense that there was a war going on inside of him. Like he was always fighting so hard to keep the pain that he held from spilling out.

I watched the street as it lay silent, waiting for something. Whether I was waiting for him to come home or to never come home at all, I wasn't sure. I ran through each scenario in my head, picturing what my life would be like in either outcome with a sort of indifference that I was growing increasingly accustomed to.

Sometimes I felt like an observer of the world around me, like all I could do was watch and no one could see or hear me. This feeling of being on the outside looking in gradually fueled my emotional detachment from the world.

The crunching of the gravel beneath the tires on my dad's truck seemed to echo loudly against the undisturbed stillness of the small town we lived in, pulling me back from my drifting thoughts.
He was home, and I was unsure about whether I was happy for that.

I made my way downstairs to sleep in their room as I often did those days because I could not sleep on my own anymore. Incessant nightmares plagued my unconscious and struck a panic in me when I would wake, dreading their return.

I watched my father's dark figure stumble into the room, using the walls as well as various items of furniture to help keep him steady. He staggered over and knelt beside me where I was seated on the couch.

"Why are you still up?"

the liquor on his breath polluted the air between us.

"I couldn't sleep, I was waiting for you to come home."

I could sense the guilt that gripped him. He seemed so diminished, so vulnerable in this drunken state. No longer the big, scary thing he would become in a rage, now he knelt before me rather weepy and pathetic.

"I'm sorry I'm so late, I'm here now though, everything is okay."

He attempted to reassure me, tripping over his words, but the words that descended fell on ears that didn't believe them anymore. It was just another broken promise. I knew that there would be more nights that he would come home drunk, and I knew that there was always a possibility of him never coming home at all.

Sometimes I wished for the latter.

***

As a kid my mom would often tell me the story of how I came to be in this world; about what an unusual arrival it was. She would weave the story in delicate detail, starting from the beginning.

She told me that after having two boys that were only two years apart-my older brothers-she felt that she was done having kids. She had always longed for a girl, but after two boys in a row she was too afraid for a third, and so she made the decision to get her tubes tied right after giving birth to my second oldest brother.

About 7 months later, to hers and everyone's surprise, she discovered that she was pregnant with me. I had been conceived and born while her tubes were tied.
I was a 0.01% chance.
Her miracle child, she would call me. I was the daughter she always yearned for.
I would peer up at her as she spoke, hanging on her every word with stars in my eyes and feeling so special. She would tell me how strong I was, how determined, how I fought for my place in this world, and I made it.

"Don't ever stop fighting."

She told me.

I was so proud of this fact, that throughout my life, I would tell everyone that I met-teachers, friends, kids at school. I would sit and contemplate how I must have had some grandiose, important purpose in this world, and that's why God made sure that I came into it.
I felt kind of like a superhero.

Somewhere along the way as I grew older, life began to build and shape walls around my heart, and the words from the beloved tale no longer sparked the same sense of joy and wonder as they always had when I was a kid.
The words felt empty, hollow.
Like they were just a fairytale, a children's story.

The way that I perceived myself, the world, my reason for being, began to shift and change.
I began to wonder that if she had gotten her tubes tied, she must have never really wanted me. One failure after

another, one mistake after another, any sense of purpose began to feel vague and distant-just beyond reach. Though I struggled to grasp it, I just couldn't understand.

I began to feel more like a mistake, than a miracle.

***

After my mom and I left the doctor's office that day, the car ride home remained void of conversation, aside from a very brief, hushed phone call that she had taken.

"Yeah, they said she's depressed."

She informed the mystery person on the other end of the line.

I moved my attention between her expression in the rearview mirror and the world outside as it raced past the window. As if we were stationary in that moment, unmoving, and the rest of the world outside passed us by.

Not having any real conception of what this word meant-depression-when I returned to school the next day, I began to repeat the story to all my friends. Regardless of the context, I felt that it was something that set me apart in what felt like a sea of uniformity. It was something that belonged to me, and no one else. It's not like there was much excitement in that little community so my diagnosis was quite the topic of conversation amongst the rest of the kids at school.

My dad seemed to hate everything about therapy and any kind of mental health related subject, so, of course, he brushed it off as "bullshit."

My mom, however, seemed to harbor more concern with what the doctor had said.

I could see that the whole ordeal, and what it could mean, often ate away at the back of her mind as she wondered to herself how it could have happened.

I don't believe I had the capacity to have any sort of understanding on whether I felt depressed, although I did carry with me a constant sense of being different and separate from my peers.

To me, the way that I felt was just the way that I felt, I had nothing else to compare it to.

Though I did have my older brothers, I often felt like an only child. We were all close in age with only a couple of years between each of us, but I had always felt disconnected from them, like we were from different planets or spoke a different language.

The whole boys are from Mars and girls are from Jupiter or whatever that childhood anecdote was.

Really, I couldn't help but feel that everyone else in the world was from Mars, and I was the singular citizen of Jupiter, lost in a sea of Martians.

***

Like any 10-year-old, I had many bright ideas. One of them being the pet rock that I adopted named Jeffrey. My second oldest brother had adopted one just like it, which he had named Henry. It wasn't unusual for kids our age to have "pet rocks," however the only difference was the rocks that we had chosen to adopt happened to be rather large, weighing around thirty pounds or so each.

Why we chose such large rocks remains a mystery.

On an otherwise unremarkable day, I had been given the task of cleaning up the playroom and picking up all the toys that lay strewn about the floor. Carefully and methodically, I picked up each one, carrying it over to the bin and dropping them in. I wondered somewhat resentfully to myself why my brothers weren't required to help, but I obliged, nonetheless.
I set my sights on Jeffrey, and, with pure determination, I squared off my feet to either side, getting my stance ready to lift the heavy stone. I managed to lift him off the ground with a great deal of effort and an audible huff and began with waddling baby steps over to the other side of the playroom.
Rather quickly, my fingers grew tired and weak, as I could feel the rock slipping from my palms. Then, in the blink of an eye, my hands were empty.
I looked down at my feet, Jeffrey had landed right on top of my right foot.

Why didn't I feel any pain?

Gingerly, I lifted him off, shoving him over to one side, and I revealed a smashed and bloody big toe underneath. I blinked at the carnage for a second or two. The lack of pain, or the shock that I was in, had left me incapable of fully registering what had happened.

I did know one thing for sure, I needed a band-aid.

Hopping on one foot, I made my way over to my brother's rooms, which sat side by side on the opposite end of the hallway from mine. The door to my second oldest brother's room was open, just enough for me to stand in the doorway. It was silent for a moment until his attention turned towards me. He looked at me, then down at my foot, bleeding on the floor, and his face took on an expression of surprise. Surprise at the extent of my injury, and surprise at my lack of reaction, probably.

"I need a band-aid."

I informed him.

"Jesus Sarah what happened?"

He asked, frantically leaping off the bed to my aid.

I explained the situation as he hurried off to the bathroom to find a band-aid and something to clean it up with.
After that day, because of the injury, my toenail fell off, and a new one eventually grew to take its place.
I "grounded" Jeffrey, banishing him to a life outside, in the garden. (He is still there to this day, I presume).

Several months later, on a quiet summer day, the world was still. The houses' skeleton creaked and groaned as the mid July sun expanded its wooden bones. I wandered from room to room, examining my family's things in my curious nature and trying to find something to occupy my mind or maybe fill the space that steadily grew within me.

After pacing around the house for a while, I eventually found myself in my parent's room, rooting through some of my mother's things as I sometimes did. I liked to look through her belongings, her wooden jewelry box with the glass door, trying on her high heel shoes and fingering through her dresses that hung in the walk-in closet just inside the master bathroom. On special occasions I was lucky enough to be able to take a swim in their large, jetted bathtub.

I stood there for a moment or two, in the silent, empty room, staring at the wooden post bedframe that held up my parent's queen-sized bed.
I thought about the time several months ago when I had hurt my toe. I thought about the attention that I had received, how I had felt cared for.
As all these considerations went through my head, I walked over to one of the corner posts of the bedframe, eyeing its sturdy physique. It was heavy, solid wood. I placed my hand on it, mulling over the idea that was forming in my mind. I wrapped both of my hands around the lip of the corner post, and with all my weight, assessed to see if I could lift it.
And I could…barely.
Setting it back on the floor, I looked again for some time, first at the bed, then at my toe.
I wondered how hard I would have to drop this bed frame on my toe to achieve a similar injury as the one I had gotten several months prior.
I wondered if I had the guts to do it.
I lifted the bed up again, positioning my toe just underneath the leg.

I slowly released my hold, though still maintaining most of its weight, and I let the bed post come to rest on top of my foot, gently this time.
It was heavy, and its weight bore down with a painful pressure.
Raising it back up, I freed my toe from underneath.

I don't think I can do it.

I felt frustrated with myself, with my lack of courage and resolve. For quite some time I stood in that room, willing myself to inflict this injury. I felt as though I needed it, and I was too stubborn to give up right away.

Don't think about it, just do it.

I desperately tried to convince myself, but after some time, I gave up.
Annoyed, I left my parent's room and retreated to my bedroom, where I lay on my bed and wished that I could cry.
The tears would not come, though.

***

I juggled the barbie dolls in my arms, attempting to keep myself from dropping any of them, as I made my way downstairs from my room, through the dining room, and outside.

God forbid I ever had to make a second trip, stubborn as I was.

Neither of my brothers looked up from the TV as I tiptoed past the living room. The sounds of the show they were watching echoed throughout the house and followed me as I made my way outside.

The sun was beating down from directly above, the air was oppressively muggy and smelled of overgrown grass and sunbaked dust. I eased myself down the splintered stairs of the stained wood deck one fragile step at a time and hobbled over to the forgotten patch of dirt that sat beside the dog kennel.

My dad had once had something planned for this spot, but I couldn't remember what it was anymore. I'm not sure he remembered either.

Glancing around, I surveyed the area for some sort of digging tool, as I let the barbies fall from my arms, plopping on the ground with a collective thud. Finding a sizeable stick, I began to dig into the earth. The soil was supple and moist, giving way easily to my excavation; it had rained a night or two before.

I was crouched there in the dirt for some time, making sure to dig a hole that would be big enough. Pausing periodically, I would eye my work, wiping sweat from my brow and smearing mud across my face in the process. I inspected the hole, turning to review the pile of barbies, and back to the hole again.

It would have to do.

I shoveled the dolls into my arms once again and stood over the freshly dug grave. With an ominous pause I stared down at the hole, then I dropped the dolls in, peering at them as they lay there for a few moments.

Time to grow up.

I thought to myself.

I wasn't sure what had brought me to this decision that I was too big to play with dolls, but I planted firm in my resolution.
I felt a deep ache in my chest, looking down at the once cherished toys, now nothing more than garbage, smudged with dirt. A sense of grief, loss, and a desire to go back to when I didn't think about things of this nature flooded my body.

With one last forlorn look at the dolls, I began to scoop the pile of dirt back over the hole, sealing the dolls into their final resting place in the ground.

***

Squinting into the glass, I intimately examined each of the smiles in the framed family picture. They all looked

so relaxed, so at ease with themselves, each other, and probably everyone else around them, too.
I couldn't help but notice the way that their eyes shone, reflecting the light from the flash of the camera, the way that their smiles pulled up, delicately creasing the skin at the corners of their faces. I couldn't help but notice how genuine they were-real happiness.

My friend's mom was a bigger lady, with a nest of heavy, bright orange hair and a jovial expression, her dad was tall and lanky, with mahogany brown hair and a full moustache set just a few inches below a pair of thick reading glasses that sat loosely atop his nose. Her brothers had inherited their dad's dark hair and lanky figure, and she was set apart from all of them with her long dirty blonde hair.
I considered my friend and her family, about the way that they were. Whether or not I meant to, or if I even realized I was doing it, I often found myself comparing their lives with mine.
I just couldn't help but notice certain things.
Usually, the things that her family had, and mine seemed to be sorely lacking.
Like the way her that parents loved each other, and the way that you could tell just by watching them together. I admired that.
Like the ease with which they interacted with each other, the way their house was filled with smells of comfort food and sounds of laughter and conversation.

Luckily for me, their picturesque two-story house was only a short walk away from mine, and I often spent time over there, as we played with our toys and imaginations and spent the nights in sleeping bags on her trampoline in the backyard.

All I had to do was make the journey across the barren field that lay between our streets, doing my best to dodge the snake holes and goat heads along the way.

She never stayed at my house, and I never asked her to.

The air and the energy were warm; the house itself felt inviting and comfortable. It always seemed to be bustling with some commotion caused by her and I and her two brothers.

Both of her brothers were older, her being the youngest and the only girl, just like me and my own brothers.

It might have been this shared life experience that sparked our friendship in the beginning, I'm not sure, but once we became friends, we were inseparable. Sometimes I liked to pretend that I was a part of their family, that her and I were sisters. I wanted to fade away from my own world and become a part of hers. Accepting this feat as one that was inescapably impossible, I decided to make do with spending as much time there as I could, instead.

I was grateful for a place to retreat where I could entertain some sense of normalcy.

***

Accompanied by nothing other than the sound of my own footsteps, I wandered through the dusty field, the sun shone unforgiving on the top of my head, warming my hair, and subtly burning the bits of scalp that were exposed.
Taking each step slowly and deliberately, I kept my eyes fixed on the ground so as not to step in any prairie dog holes along the way. A twisted ankle was the last thing I needed.
I would pause, every so often, picking up rocks or sticks or whatever happened to catch my eye, and placing them in my pocket if I deemed them worthy of keeping.
By myself, in silence, just wandering the Earth.

Hadn't I always been this way?

I poked around the yard for a while until I got to the white, plastic picket fence that lined our two ½-acre property and I carefully slipped in between the bottom two posts, retreating down the hill towards the creek that ran there. Taking each step cautiously so as not to slide down the embankment, I came to rest on a small boulder next to the creek.
Wielding one of the sticks that I had picked up along the way, I jabbed around the water, flipping over rocks, and fishing out stray weeds that were caught in the current, floating down the stream. The sound of the creek water rushing made me feel calm, at peace.
Anywhere outside, really, and I felt more at peace.

I sat there in silence for quite some time, alone with my thoughts and the inner workings of my imagination. I sat

there long enough for the sun to pass over me, over the trees, as it came to rest atop the peaks of the mountains, casting shadows along their curves, a chill settling in the air as the sky grew darker.
I wanted to sit there forever.
Just exist there in the silence and the serenity.
I felt a chill run up my back and my skin pimpled up as a breeze rolled by and I saw something move out of the corner of my eye.
Startled, I looked up.

Perched on a small rock, about twenty feet away from me, was a cat. It looked like a younger cat, perhaps similar in cat years to my own early age. Lost somewhere in between child and adult, whirling through time and space into unwelcomed teenage years.

I must have surprised it as well, for it sat there, unmoving, just staring at me.
I called after it, hoping it would come to me, but it maintained its position, statuesque in the afternoon dusk.

"Go home, Sarah."

A clear and distinctive thought ran through my head.

I glanced back at the place that I dreaded returning to, and back again to where the cat had been.
The cat was gone.

I felt sorrow for the space that was left in its place, and I wished with all my heart that it would take me away wherever it had gone to.

With a great, surrendering sigh, I felt the tiniest bit of my stubborn nature escape my body with my breath. I reluctantly picked myself up and made my way home.

***

My father was in a drunken rage again, like a tornado ripping its way through the house, tearing to pieces every little thing that stood in its path.

This fight felt much worse than all the ones that had come before it. As if every argument and all the long nights spent in screaming matches were all leading up to this-the grand finale

The tension in the house was palpable, the air thick with fear and emotion.

My brothers and I were seated at the dining room table. For whatever reason, my dad was sure that he did not want us to retreat to our rooms this time. We sat there as we were told, with our heads hung low, glancing at each other nervously with tearful eyes, unsure of what was going to come of all this.

We watched as my mom would storm from one room to the next, trying to get away from him and he would follow her where she went, for this fight wasn't over until he said so.

I studied the knots engrained in the wooden table, trying to lose myself in the pattern.

Usually, I could slip away into my thoughts and drown out what was happening around me, but on this night, fear held me in place.

I was frozen, stuck.

My mom, feeling defeated and exhausted, retreated outside to smoke a cigarette on the deck and take a breath and a break from the war.

My dad went over to the door that she had walked out of and locked it, muttering some profanities about filthy cigarettes and how the people that smoked them were just as filthy.

As he did this, he turned and looked at me dead in the eye and said,

"If you unlock that door, I will beat the shit out of you."

I just looked back at him in silence as he stomped away.

Scared as I was of my father, I got up to unlock the door the moment that he disappeared out of the room. I could not just leave my mother out there.

"Sarah, don't."

My brothers looked at me nervously, pleading for me not to for fear of angering our dad even more. They, too, were unsure of what he would do.
I ignored their pleas, and I hurriedly flipped the latch and sat back down at the table. I stared down at my hands in my lap, wishing that this would all be over.

I wondered what my friend and her family were doing at that very same moment.

With this thought came the great feeling of loss of that life which I had never had.

After getting some air and letting her tears dry, my mom finished her smoke and came back inside. Her presence in the house once again launched my father into a fit. They were standing in the kitchen, and my dad ordered my brothers and I to stand up and join them.

He was yelling at all of us to stop crying, which in turn, made us cry even more.

I'm not sure what he was trying to prove to us by making us witness the argument. Maybe he thought that we would see that he was right to be mad and it was my mom that was wrong.
Rage boiled beneath his eyes, the sounds of him screaming blended with the sounds of my brothers and I sobbing until it was one great symphony of chaos.
He was not my father when he was drunk like this.
The charismatic, fun, and humorous man that he could be, nowhere to be found, replaced instead by a broken soul, incapable of expressing the hurt in any other way than with rage.

I flinched as he flung the beer bottle that he was holding at the kitchen cabinet beside us, and it shattered into pieces with a crash that reverberated throughout the entire house.
The sound of the breaking glass seemed to wake him from his black out.

All at once, the house fell silent.

Blinking away the stupor and confusion, he looked around at all of us, at the shards of the broken bottle that lay strewn all over the floor and, stunned, he fell to his knees. He began to cry and hug each one of us in his arms as he repeated over and over,

"I'm so sorry."

That was the night that my mother had finally had enough. My dad slept in the playroom that doubled as a guest room, and my brothers and I spent the night on the floor of my parent's room with my mom in her bed. We were all exhausted from the flood of emotions and we did not speak much about any of it, but we all knew without having to say it aloud that everything was going to change.

The household moved forward in the way that one might walk over broken glass. The air was riddled with hurt feelings, resentment, and shame. What was broken could not be fixed anymore, nor could it be ignored.
It went on this way for a few months- my parents sleeping separately as the divorce was finalized and my mom came up with a plan of where we were going to go.

Other members of my family and some of the other kids at school often asked me if I were okay regarding the divorce and the upcoming move and I did not understand why they would ask these questions.

I was more than okay.

I was relieved.

***

2

Later that year, during the early days of summer, my family and I were out to dinner to celebrate my 12th birthday, and, as usual, my parents struggled to be civil with one another throughout the duration of the meal. My mom, brothers, and I were about to move to a new town, where we would all start anew. Happy as I was to be away from my father, I was sad to leave my friends and all that I had known.

Taking our seats around the table in a small Italian restaurant, I braced myself for an uncomfortable evening. I sat on the end, spending much of the time with my eyes lowered and pushing my food around my plate.

My parents argued throughout the night, making jabs and snide comments at any opportunity they could get, and my brothers conversed mostly with each other, occasionally turning their attention towards me to ask a question or two.

I didn't have much of an appetite at that point-mostly I just wanted to get out of there so I could be alone.

Every so often I would look up from my task of pushing the food around my plate and survey the people around me, wondering to myself what their lives might be like. I frequently found my sight caught on an older couple that were sat across the restaurant. They appeared to be somewhere in their seventies or eighty's. A man with a kind, forgettable face, and a gentle looking woman with stark white hair and a brightly colored blouse adorned with flowers. They looked just like anyone's grandparents would look, nothing out of the ordinary, but I couldn't seem to pull my attention away from their presence.

I noticed them glancing over at me throughout the night, speaking softly to each other-a conversation that I could not hear.

The sound of my parents fighting eventually faded to the back of my mind as it always did.

I kept my attention on the older couple. They were not familiar to me; I could not think of who they were, though they looked at me as though they knew me.

My curiosity was peaked, and my vivid imagination took ahold of the situation; I dove into the moment within my mind and spent the remainder of dinner there.

The evening dragged on in a slow and painful crawl and just as my dad was hailing for the check, I watched as the older couple slowly got up to leave. They made their way across the restaurant exchanging quiet words with one another, and on their way out they passed by our table.

When they walked by me, they placed a note on the table in front of me. We met eyes for an extended moment but without a word they left the carefully folded piece of paper before me and disappeared out the door.

My family fell silent as they all turned and looked at me. They were as puzzled as I was, and they all simultaneously began asking me what the note said, and who those people were-as if I had any clue.

Meeting their inquiries with shrugging shoulders and a silently shaking head, I carefully unfolded the mystery note to reveal the words:

"Happy Birthday Sarah
-from us"

I studied each word carefully, the way they wrote "Happy Birthday Sarah" in big bubble letters, the way "from us" was underlined with a zigzag line in the bottom right corner of the note. I stared at it for some time, blinking in disbelief and wonder.

How did they know my name, or that it was my birthday?

I knew for certain that they were a far enough distance away in the restaurant that there was no way that they could have overheard any conversations being had by my family and me.
I passed the note to my brother who was seated next to me, and he studied it, and the rest of my family did the same as they passed it around the table.
Each one of us buzzed with the same questions.

Who were those people?
Did any of us know them?
Why did they leave this note?

We left the restaurant that evening just as the sun was slipping from the darkening sky. The air was warm and smelled like a fresh rain was falling somewhere in the distance. For a moment everything felt okay. The arguments of the evening were long forgotten and the elated feeling of receiving the note lingered on within me.

I felt as though someone finally saw me, rather than looked at or through me.

I concluded for myself that it did not matter who those people were, or why they left the note.

I was just grateful to be seen.

***

The time between when my parents decided to separate and when we moved away from my dad felt to me as though it dragged on forever. There were so many hurt feelings that flooded the air and so many words left unsaid. Between the lines of the words that *were* spoken there was so much heartache and regret.
Although, the fighting did slow down a lot.
It was as if they were just too exhausted to even try to be angry anymore.
After the separation and divorce became finalized, my mom packed herself, my brothers and I up and moved us to another city-a fresh start. The school there was rated one of the best in the country and it was quite a respectable place to live so it seemed suitable enough.

When the day finally came, my brothers and I all piled in the car, and I stared out the window in silence as everything we had ever known slowly disappeared behind us.
Moving away from this house and town that I grew up in was difficult, but I was happy for the fighting to be over. My brothers always seemed to make friends easily, so I suspected that they weren't worried about the new school. Myself, being the shy and quiet kid that I was, had a tough time imagining how to make new friends.
I had never had to do so before.

That first day of school, I was incredibly nervous. I cowered behind my second oldest brother as we stood in the extensive line of students waiting to enter the school and find our way to orientation.
He began chatting with a few kids his age, and they quickly warmed up to each other. I watched their interactions as if I were studying some alien species. Feeling a sense of separation more than ever, I realized just how much I didn't understand or relate to other people.

I never felt like I knew how to talk like them, think like them, or act like them. Though I always did my best to put on my mask and pretend.
Despite my awkward nature I managed to find myself immersed in a group of girls who took me under their wing. I was flattered by their kindness. I was also intimidated by how pretty and cool everyone there was. It was so different, and so much bigger than the small town and quaint school that I was used to.

I hung around with this same group of girls for most of the year and one of them became my best friend.
About halfway through the year, for what seemed to be no reason at all, her and I simultaneously went off in a direction of rebellion. I had cut my hair and began wearing heavy eye makeup, (which my dad made me scrub off my face every time he saw it). I found myself drawn to the "hardcore scene"-the kids who listened to metal and styled their hair into colorful mullets.
I felt resentments growing inside of me towards the people around me. I resented that they were rich and

well off, while I watched my mom struggle to support us.

I resented how effortlessly pretty the girls were, how all the boys liked them and how they fit in with ease.

My family, teachers, everyone around me struggled to understand what it was that was going on with me, and I did not have the words to tell them.

The truth was, I barely knew what was going on with me at that time, either.

I returned home from school as I did any other day. Meeting my mom's greeting with a silent glance, I bounded up the stairs, eager to be alone. Tossing my backpack on my bed and kicking off my shoes, I made my way into the office, and I logged on to the computer to begin my afternoon routine of wading through the internet.

Listening to music and browsing through my social media, I was suddenly pulled away from the screen when my phone rang.

It was somewhere around the end of May, and I had only about a week and half of school left before the year was over.

"Hello?"

I instantly recognized my friend's distraught voice on the other end, and I listened intently to each word as she fumbled over her own sobbing.

"They found the list."

In those four words, I knew exactly what she was referring to. Earlier that day, we had spent our seventh period class sitting together and writing this list of people that we went to school with.
Jokingly, the top of the paper read,

<u>People I'm Going to Drown in my Bathtub</u>

I tried to wrap my head around what she was saying as she explained that they were having a meeting about whether to expel us. I felt like I was in a bad dream and at any moment I would be jolted awake. It felt like a sick joke.
At the direction of her parents, we couldn't see or speak to each other anymore.
I didn't say much for the entire phone call if anything at all.
When she was done informing me of our inevitable fate, she hurriedly ended the phone call, not wanting her parents to find out that she was talking to me.
I hung up and stared blankly at the wall.
Everything she had told me bounced around my head like a pinball and I struggled to keep up with my brain's attempt to process it.
My heart felt like an anchor, crushed by the weight of the ocean as it sunk. I could hear it beating in my ears and my stomach began to turn.

Not too long after I had hung up the phone, the police arrived at our front door. I followed my mom's voice as she called me downstairs, and I sat on the couch in a daze as they asked me questions about the list. My eyes

fixed on the floor, so heavy with shame that I could not lift them to meet anyone's gaze.
Everything around me fell away and there was nothing but me and my thoughts in that moment.
I fought to understand how this could have happened.

It must have fallen out of my binder, but how?

Every possible scenario raced through my head as I felt sheer terror and utter vulnerability knowing that the rest of my life was in the hands of those teachers and staff that were sitting in that room-deciding what my fate would be.

After some hours of deliberation and debate, they had reached a verdict; regardless of if they felt it was necessary, they concluded that they had to do something-they could not just let it go.

I was expelled.

The next week or so was nothing more than a blur as I struggled to stay present, but my reality was just too painful. My parents alternated between anger at the situation and fear for me. They tried their best to reassure me that everything would be okay.
Their attempts at comfort seemed hollow, and I sensed that they did not believe their own words even as they said them.
I would wander from room to room in the house, trying my best to ignore the hushed conversations between my parents. They weren't sure what to do, or how to help.

They decided that it would be best for me to stay at my dad's house for a little while, to get away from everything. I neither agreed nor disagreed, I just did what they asked, numb and functioning on a sort of autopilot state.

I packed up several changes of clothes and a few essential belongings and loaded them into my dad's truck. Taking my place in the front seat, I clicked my seatbelt on and stared out the window at the house.

It didn't feel like home.

About a week had slipped by staying at my dad's. My time spent there was mostly filled with me watching TV and him making numerous, desperate attempts to help me feel better. I recognized his effort, and I knew how much he cared about me, but I couldn't shake the gut-wrenching feeling that had lingered since the day that the whole thing started. I spent a lot of time staring blankly at the TV, not paying attention but rather replaying the events of that day repeatedly in my head, hating myself and God for letting this happen.

On the night before my 13th birthday, he offered to order us pizza and left me in the living room to eat and watch movies as he retired for the evening. I was full of remorse, I knew that he just wanted me to be happy, but all I wanted was to disappear. Happiness no longer seemed like a possibility at that time. I could not see past the darkness that surrounded me.

I had made up my mind and I made my way to the bathroom, searching the medicine cabinet for whatever I could find to end my life.
My parents had suspected my suicidal ideology at this point so most everything was locked away; however, being committed to the cause, I grabbed the only thing I could find-a bottle of ibuprofen.
I poured out a handful of the round, rust colored pills and stared at them for maybe a second or two before I proceeded to take them several at a time. Standing in front of the mirror, I would take several, wash them down, and repeat. I watched my reflection as I did this, staring at the girl in front of me.
I felt nothing.
After finishing off what was in the bottle, I went back to my seat on the couch and curled up within the blankets and closed my eyes.

I woke up almost 12 hours later, on my birthday.
My family was there, unsuspecting of the intended suicide attempt.
They had brought presents and a desperate attempt at giving me a normal birthday and, feeling a sense of obligation, I humored my family, opened the presents, and hung out for a while.
My dad emerged from the kitchen, proudly wielding the cake in his hands. A smile on his face and sadness in his eyes, he made his way into the living room and set it down in front of me, lighting the candles.

I stared at the flickering flames and as everyone told me to make a wish,

I wished that I were dead.

***

Not surprisingly, I had no friends at this point.
The school had called all the parents on the "list" and let them know what had happened, "just in case," I supposed.
I was ostracized from not only the school, but the entire town.
Everyone knew who I was, and not in the way that anyone would ever want to be known.
The sense of loneliness that existed within me was a yawning void that threatened to swallow me whole at any given moment.
I did my best to make it through the days.

As New Year's Eve rolled around, there were a couple of girls from my old school that for whatever reason, still accepted me as a human being.

They had invited me over to their house for the holiday, just the three of us.
I was so excited to have somewhere to go and a group to belong to I struggled to maintain my composure as I packed an overnight bag and got ready to leave.
My mother acknowledged this glimmer of hope in me, and I think it sparked some hope in her as well.
I knew how much she worried about me, and I felt powerless to put any of her fears at ease, for they were my fears as well.

I spent the car ride over in a giddy state, too excited to be bothered by the frostbitten air.
We arrived at the girl's house, and my mom gave me a hug and wished me well for the evening.

"Have fun."

I heard her pull away as my friend came to the door to let me in.
I had never hung out with her before, so I felt a little out of sorts, but her kindness in inviting me had put my anxiety somewhat at ease.
We spent the evening listening to music and talking, drinking sparkling cider from champagne glasses, and discussing the latest gossip.
Addressing the elephant in the room, we discussed what had happened at school, and they expressed their sympathy for what had happened.

"I don't think it was fair what happened."

They remarked.

I was grateful to hear that not everyone in town thought that I was bad.
At one point or another my friend's mom had poked her head in the door to check on us, and my friend introduced me.

"It's nice to meet you, Sarah."

She greeted me.
She left us to our festivities after the brief introductions.
Not too long after the initial greeting, she came back in and asked to speak with her daughter privately.
My friend left the room, while the other girl and I sat in mostly silence.

There was some part of my intuition that sensed what was coming, but maybe I just didn't want to believe it.

My friend returned, visibly upset.
She was angry and near tears, as she explained to me that her mother had said that I needed to leave.
After learning my name and putting the pieces together of who I was, she had decided that she didn't want me around her daughter.
I was in shock, mortified, and full of shame.
It was somewhere around 10:30 PM when I made the phone call to my mom to come pick me up.
She was so angry with the situation that she couldn't get the words out to express it, and with a heavy sigh she agreed to come get me.

"I'm so sorry, I had no idea she would actually do something like this."

My friend was over-remorseful, apologizing repeatedly, desperate to help me feel even a little bit better about the situation. I assured her it was okay, as I packed my overnight bag to return home. My cheeks were burning with embarrassment, and I struggled to hold back the tears.
Climbing into my mother's car, she looked at me with heartbreak and worry as I slumped down in the seat.
We drove home in silence, and I watched the lights fly by the windows.
A new year was almost here, and my hopes for anything to be different were nowhere to be found.
I retreated to my room, my bed, and I let the void of loneliness pull me into a deep sleep filled with nightmares.

***

The first time that I ever got drunk, I drank so much that I blacked out and passed out in the grass at the park.

I was with a girl from my soccer team-this sport being the only thing I had left of a normal teenage experience. I was quite good at it, though my newfound habit of smoking cigarettes had left me unable to keep pace as I had before.

We were at her parent's house, listening to music and sitting on the kitchen floor, the sunlight shining through the windows and illuminating the room.
For whatever reason or perhaps no reason at all-one of us had an idea. (It was probably me).

We rummaged through her parent's liquor cabinet-which they kept right in the kitchen, unlocked. They obviously trusted their well-to-do daughter.
Maybe I *was* the bad influence. Or, at least, I was becoming one.
Finding a bottle of alcohol that didn't sound or smell too awful to stomach, we took turns taking swigs straight from the bottle. It was banana flavored vodka, and though it burned my throat and stomach it filled me with a sense of ease and warmth that I latched onto almost immediately.
While my friend had stopped after a couple of drinks, a fire was lit within me. An insatiable thirst to pursue the feeling that the alcohol gave me was awakened, and I wanted more. And more.
I don't remember how much I drank, and it was somewhere during my time there on the kitchen floor that I drank myself into a black out.
The next thing I knew I semi-awakened from my autopilot state to find myself and my friend walking down to the park by her house.
Well, she was walking, I was stumbling while she struggled to keep me on my feet.
She had decided that it was too risky to stay at her house, if her parents had come home to find me like that, she would be in for it.

So, we shuffled off to the park and walked until I apparently could walk no more, and I collapsed in the grass under the shade of a maple tree.
I don't know how long we were there for, but my friend stayed with me as I slept off the booze, to make sure that I was okay. At one point I roused from my drunken stupor to find two guys with us. I did not know when they had gotten there or how long any of us had been there, and I struggled to maintain consciousness as I drifted in and out of the conversation that surrounded me.
Eventually, I was awake enough to call my mom, and she came and picked me up,
I watched her car pull up to the curb, and I swallowed the feelings of fear as I knew I was still nowhere near sober enough to face her.
But I had no choice.
Pathetically, I crawled into her car, and I lay in the back seat, the world around spinning too fast for me to remain upright.
My mom knew right away that something was wrong, and I knew that a scolding awaited me, but I was too drunk to care.

***

3

It appeared that I was at odds with the world around me, as well as the world within me.

I felt as though I was merely drifting from one day to the next. Often wishing for death but lacking any real resolve to see it through, I felt that I was being punished and made to stay here and suffer.

Drugs and alcohol crept their way into my life more, as I desperately sought out any means to turn the world within, and without, off.

I found myself at a new school not too far away from the previous one-they had agreed to take me in after my expulsion.

Making new friends ceased to be much of an option at this point as everyone knew who I was and what I had done.

Outcasted and ostracized, I felt the many eyes that stared at me as I wandered through the unchanging hallways day after day.

Sitting in art class one day, I kept to myself, and doodled in my notebook as usual. I was pulled from my own inner world when a girl that I did not recognize came and sat next to me. I couldn't help but notice how pretty she was, and when she started talking to me, I could hardly believe it. There was no doubt in my mind that she was popular, or would be once people met her, and I wondered silently to myself what interest she could possibly have in me-the school outcast.

From an outside perspective we appeared to be polar opposites-my hair was dyed black and I always wore heavy black makeup-but on the inside we were very much the same, and we quickly became best friends. I

always had this idea that she took me in. She was exceptionally beautiful, the kind of beautiful that people feel drawn to and want to be around.
I felt a sense of victory that she had chosen me to be her best friend, since I had spent what felt like so long being alone.
We spent all our free time together and would get ready in her room for whatever party was happening that weekend, music blasting through the speakers. I regarded her as a light in the vast, dark sea that I had been lost in for so long.

Somehow, I had managed to make it to April, a little over halfway through the school year. My mom was taking me to my weekly psychiatrist appointment after school and on this day, I had some exciting news to share.

I typically had a challenging time focusing due to my depression despite the various medications they had been trying to place me on, and a few days earlier I had accepted a pill of Adderall from an acquaintance in hopes that it would help me get through midterms that week.
To my surprise, it helped me a great deal. I looked forward to exploring this possibility with my doctor. Countless times before this, they had put me on medications that either did nothing or made it worse, so I was happy to have found something that made a positive difference in my life.
It felt like a glimmer of hope.

I sat in the small room in a chair across from the psychiatrist, tearing threads off my ripped jeans and rolling them up into tiny balls, stacking them in a neat little pile on my lap.
I was always careful not to make eye contact during therapy, and I would just awkwardly hang my head and respond with one-or-two-word sentences as she would fire off questions, her eyes boring into my psyche.
She was not the kind of woman that would ever make me feel at ease. Middle aged and ever so slightly overweight, chestnut brown hair cut short, a curt expression on her face, she was the opposite of warm and welcoming.

We talked about my week, and I eagerly reported to her what had happened with the medication. I explained to her how much it had helped me, and I asked her if it would be possible to evaluate me to see if that might be something we could look into-my own prescription.
Her face remained void of expression, as usual, and she quietly nodded and assured me that we could talk about it next time, as we were nearing the end of our session that day.
I left her office feeling hopeful. None of the many antidepressants they had thrown at me had ever seemed to help I looked forward to trying something new.
My mom and I drove home, ate dinner, and that night I fell fast asleep.

I awoke the next morning like any other day, got ready and left for school.
I wasn't there for more than an hour when I was called into the principal's office. This wasn't necessarily an

unusual occurrence for me; I was always finding myself right in the middle of whatever trouble was around. I had a smart mouth and an attitude, and it had me in battle with the teachers on more than one occasion.

I did not think anything of it.

I walked into the room and immediately my gaze fell upon two police officers that were already there. The principal was seated in his chair, and the officers were standing, one on either side of the desk, their hands resting on their belts.
My heart sank into the pit of my stomach as I met eyes with each of the people in the room.

What was this about?

They requested that I sit down, and silently I obliged. Sparing the small talk and wasting no time, they promptly began interrogating me.
They asked me about the Adderall, where I had gotten it, things like that.
I answered their questions one after the other-my stomach sinking into my shoes.
I could not believe that this was happening.
I wished they would stop looking at me the way that they were- like a criminal, a degenerate.
I had only one question for them when all was said and done:

How did they find out about this?

They explained to me rather casually that my psychiatrist had called and reported the incident shortly after I had left her office the day before.
The one person betrayed me who was-by law-meant to keep my confidence.
I felt sick to my stomach and felt myself detaching from my reality as they explained to me that I was to be expelled from school once more and charged with felony drug possession for the one pill of Adderall that was in my system.

This can't be real.

I willed myself to wake up from this nightmare, but to no avail. I was very much awake, this was very much my life, and I felt completely trapped.

I was escorted off school property in handcuffs by the officers. Tears streamed hot down my cheeks as I hung my head in shame and embarrassment. Everyone's eyes felt like daggers in my chest and in my back as they turned to watch me being taken out of school.
The officers walked me over to where my mom anxiously waited, biting her fingernails as she stood by the car. I couldn't help but notice how sad she looked. Her heart broke for me as she wondered what would become of me.
I got into her car, and she probed me with questions about what happened. I didn't want to answer them, it didn't really matter anymore.

Nothing mattered anymore. The walls that I was building grew evermore as I locked myself away, determined to protect myself from an unrelentingly cruel world. I shut everyone out and I shut myself down.

I stared out the window as the houses and cars and trees raced by, blending into each other as we made our way back home.

I felt my heart shrink even further, until it was so small and so buried that I could barely feel it anymore.

***

I wanted to be anyone but me, anywhere but home, and so I began to run away frequently, wanting to escape the actuality of my life. I never went all that far and was usually found by my parents or police and taken against my will back to my house as my family struggled to control what I was becoming, ripping through my life and the lives of those around me, leaving a trail of destruction in my wake.

During this time that I was not in school due to being expelled, I often found myself trapped within the confines of my home. I paced throughout the house, restless, wanting to get out. My mother was in the kitchen keeping an eye on the back door as my brother sat on the couch in the living room watching the front door.

I felt like a caged animal. I had to get out.

Rather than accept my fate, I decided that my best option was to drop out of the two-story window upstairs. Terrified of heights but determined to be free, I crawled out of the window and hung, suspended on the ledge for quite some time, afraid to let go.

Eventually I realized there was no other choice, and I released my grip on the windowsill, dropping onto the pavement below.

I was free.

I made my way to my usual hang out spot downtown and found the group of outcasts I had befriended some time before. They understood me, they knew what it was like to be rejected by society and chronically misunderstood. When I was with them, I could live out my dream of being someone else.

We drank, partied, and I met a guy a few years older than me. I was smitten, and I vowed to follow him where he went. And I did.

I spent the next several days with him in another city. I turned my phone off so that I could not be reached or found. I could never see more than a few hours in front of me, so what exactly my plan was to be I did not know.

The thought never crossed my mind.

Just so long as I was away from home and with him it didn't really matter to me.

We spent most of the time that I was there drinking, smoking weed, and hanging out at the park by his house. I felt like I belonged there, more so than anywhere else in my life.

A few days into my impromptu adventure, guilt took over and I decided I should call my mom just to let her know that I was alive.

She answered the phone before the first ring even reached completion and I could hear the panic in her voice.

My heart ached for the way that I was hurting her, but the thing was-my heart ached when I was there too, and so did hers. I truly felt that we were both better off just letting me go.

I could not see why she didn't understand that I had to get away.

I told her I was okay, but that I wasn't coming home,

"I can't"

I replied as she begged me to come back.

I listened to her cry for as long as my heart could take when I finally hung up the phone.
I walked back over to where my new friends were and began to drink to numb the pain. I loved my mom; I didn't want her to cry for me.

I just couldn't be the daughter or the person they wanted me to be.

After several days, we decided to return to our regular hang out spot and we hopped on the bus downtown. Not a care in the world, we walked hand and hand down the street. The sun was shining brightly, and the air was crisp and warm that morning.
Suddenly and serendipitously, someone that was riding their bike quite literally ran into me. I gathered my balance and looked up to apologize to the stranger when my heart stopped.

It was my father.

He grabbed me tightly by the arm as if in fear that I would turn and run away again and told me to say goodbye to my friends. As he dragged me along, I stole one last look back at my friends and my new love interest as he hurried me off to his truck. I didn't want to leave them.

I was furious and I cried the whole way home. As it turned out, my dad had been riding his bike through the town for hours every day looking for me and he had finally found me.

When we pulled up to the house there were multiple cars outside. Walking inside, I looked up to see my grandma, my uncle, my mom, and my brothers all there, seated on the couches in the living room, anxiously awaiting my safe return.
There was no yelling, no cursing, no scolding.
Everyone was just relieved that I was okay.

Sensing that I could use a break from the emotional backlash, my uncle and I took a trip to the gas station, and after some convincing on my part, he reluctantly agreed to buy me a pack of cigarettes. We sat side by side on the curb next to his truck and we talked while I smoked, and I was grateful for his understanding and compassion for my situation.
He didn't judge me, and I was grateful for that too. He simply asked me questions to piece together what was going on inside my head. It seemed that was something that everyone often wondered, and I never really had an answer for them.
When we returned to the house, we sat as a family and talked about what was to be done. I was out of control and spiraling down at an alarming rate, though it did not feel that way to me.
I just wanted to do what I wanted to do, when I wanted to do it, and I had a complete lack of respect or regard for the way things were "supposed to be."

None of us had any semblance of the right answer, but we landed on the decision that I would willingly enter myself into a mental hospital to be evaluated.
I agreed to go and accept the help they were offering. I didn't want to be the way that I was, I just couldn't stop.

I spent a little over a week in the hospital, though I don't believe it made much of a difference for me. We would sit in groups most of the day and they would ask us to rate how happy we were on a scale of 1-10.
The thing was, I didn't necessarily know what it meant to be happy. I had just felt the way that I felt for so long that the pain and anger became my normal state of being. I stared blankly at the sheet of paper in front of me, examining the row of faces that depicted a scale from depressed to happy, and settled on a three before handing it in to the counselor, retreating to my room.
It wasn't so bad all in all, my roommate there was cool, and it felt we were the only semi-sane people in there at the time. We would read the weird little scribblings that were on the walls of the room and laugh about how bat-shit crazy people were. I didn't get much help there, but I did get a nice little vacation.
It was an all too short break from life.
I sensed that there was something wrong with me, but I wasn't crazy like some of those people that I was in with, that much I knew for sure.

It was just as if I looked at the world around me and my vision was skewed. I was convinced that no one was happy, that everyone was just getting by and pretending. The world around me felt fake, and I felt disconnected from the people in it.

I made the decision that I did not want what everyone else had, I did not want their plastic smiles and the way they pretended to be nice to you only to stab you in the back. I did not want the way that people hurt one another, the lack of compassion and regard for human life.
I didn't want the job that everyone hated, the family everyone resented, the way that we all just pretended to be okay with things that were not okay.
I had no foresight to how my actions were shaping my future, and I was too stubborn to listen to the warnings of those around me. I had been hurt by too many adults at this point to ever consider the possibility that they might have my best interests in mind.

It was me against the world.

I spent the rest of that summer attending summer school so that I wouldn't fall behind and I could enter high school with the rest of my age group.
I didn't really know where I was headed, and I didn't really care.

***

My eyes began to peel open to reveal the dark and quiet room that stretched out around me. Slowly, I began to wake, wiping the crust away from the corners of my eyes and mouth, rapidly blinking away the fog that was settled over my mind.

I sat up, carefully, so as not to stir the nausea within my stomach.

I was confused.

Where was I?

I looked around me, at the sleeping figures that were scattered about the floor.

What time was it?

I thought about the night before, the rave that I had been to.

I remembered the beginning of the night, but not the end. My memory ended somewhere around the time that I had made it into the venue and was being fed pills by a guy that I had met.

Luckily, I recognized some of the people who were asleep, so I knew that I had left with the same people with whom I had arrived.

What happened though? How did we get here?

My brain slowly and lazily struggled to pick up the pieces of the night before, as I tried to stifle the bile that was churning in my gut.
I wanted to go home.

Fuck, I needed a cigarette.

I carefully stepped over the snoring bodies and stumbled over to the wall to plug my phone into the outlet.
Waiting for it to turn on, I glanced around the room again, wondering to myself how I got here. I thought maybe if I thought long and hard enough that I might remember something, but I only drew a blank.
I fished a cigarette out of my purse and lit it, as the haze began to lift from my brain.
My heart sunk when my phone turned on and I saw what time it was.
Four in the afternoon.
I had slept for the entire day. My mom was going to kill me.
My phone began to light up with text messages and voicemails, all of which I ignored, scrolling down to my brother's number, and calling him.

"Can you come pick me up?"

I implored the voice on the other end of the line.

After some initial frustration, he agreed.

I wandered out to the street to figure out where exactly I was and gave him the cross streets and house address. I was twenty miles from home, in another city.

Whose house was this?

I guess it didn't really matter anyways.

"I'll be there soon."

He promised.

The sun was just beginning to settle down over the horizon amidst the darkening atmosphere; the air was brittle on the skin and sharp in the lungs. It was the dead of winter, and the once stretched-out days of summer were condensed into short, bleak windows of time where the sun would occasionally make an appearance from behind the grey, cloud covered sky.
I stood outside for a while, watching my breath form tiny ice crystals in the air, and feeling rather hollowed out by the drugs from the night before as I waited for my brother to come rescue me.
Like a knight in shining Chrysler he finally arrived, pulling up to the curb in front of me.
I pulled the door open, and I slunk into the passenger seat.

"Where were you? Whose house is this?"

He began grilling me as soon as I got in.

Feeling too exhausted to answer any questions, I lay my head back on the seat and closed my eyes. My brother sighed with disappointment, and we drove the rest of the way in silence. I drifted in and out of a light sleep.
After what felt like a short while, something unbeknownst to me roused me from my nap. It was dark out.

Was I dreaming?

The world that lay before me had slowed to a crawl, it looked like we were moving in slow motion.
I quickly gathered that we were still in the car, but we were driving on the sidewalk, and we were heading straight for the stoplight pole at the intersection.

Was this real?

That moment seemed to last for both a lifetime, and only a split second all at once, and when we grazed the first pole of the intersection, suddenly everything sped up again and I could hear my brother screaming.
The car began spinning rapidly in circles as we whirled across the street until we slammed into the second pole, bouncing off the metal surface and coming to a final halt in the middle of the street.
The world fell silent as the car hissed and groaned from the impact.
I was in shock.

What just happened?

I looked over at my brother, who was checking both of us for any wounds.
Neither of us had been wearing a seatbelt.

"Sarah are you okay? Oh my God."

My brother was hysterical.
I was too stunned to say much except,

"I'm okay, I'm okay."

We both got out of the car, and the sight of the damage to the vehicle made me sick to my stomach.
The car was completely smashed.
Sirens wailed off in the distance as the police made their way towards us.

"I'm so sorry, I don't know what happened."

My brother kept apologizing over and over.

The rest of the night went on in a blur of police lights and people telling us how lucky we were to be alive. My brother had fallen asleep at the wheel, and we had sped up to about 70 MPH based on the damage to the car and had slammed into two stop light poles.
Neither of us had a single scratch on us.

All I could think about was how scared I was of how my parents would react.

"Dad's going to kill me."

My brother sobbed.

***

My parents didn't know what do to, and therapy seemed a final effort for me, but anything was worth a shot. Sitting by and doing nothing while I destroyed my life and myself were not an option, apparently.
Seated upon the couch in the therapist's office, the apprehension within me seeped over the brim, spilling onto the floor. I watched as it spread throughout the entire room.

I focused intently on my fidgeting hands, stealing the occasional glance up at her face to find her watching me with patient curiosity.
Whenever I looked someone in the eyes, I often felt invaded, uncomfortable. Though I never seemed to know what it was that I feared so much. Maybe I was afraid that someone would see through my walls and into the darkness and pain and decide to lock me away for good.
She was different though, the way she looked at me. Patient, kind, understanding. She looked at me as though

she really wanted to hear what I was feeling, as though she only wanted to help. I was grateful for her, though her genuine concern and attention felt like a foreign concept to me.
After experimenting with multiple different therapists my mom and I finally landed on her, and I was glad for that. I had a great deal of difficulty in building trust with them after what had happened with my second expulsion.

That day, we talked for a while about how my week had been, and she asked me her usual questions.

"Did you cut yourself this week?"

I flicked my eyes up nervously and felt a biting sense of shame as she maintained her calm and unassuming eye contact.
I nodded my head yes, returning my gaze to my lap.

"Can I see?"

She asked me.

I sensed that her question was out of concern for my well-being rather than morbid curiosity and so I obliged. I tenderly rolled up my sleeve, careful not to reinjure the wound on my arm.
Feeling childish, I carefully pulled up my sleeve and stuck my arm out for her to see, like a really twisted version of show-and-tell.
She inspected the wound in silence, nodding her head sympathetically.

She didn't ask me anything more about it after that, for which I was grateful.
I hated talking to people about my cutting, or admitting it at all, really. I wore long sleeves every day, regardless of the weather, to avoid any unwanted attention.
The thing that people failed to understand was that I wasn't trying to kill myself. Self-harm became a sort of release for me.
At times I felt as though the pain and emotions inside of me would tear me into pieces to make room for themselves and fill up a larger space. My body often seemed too small to hold all of them in at once.
I would sit on the floor of my bedroom, sinking the cold metal blade of a pair of scissors into my flesh, relishing the sharp and shocking pain. I would continue to run the blade over the wound until it opened just enough that a warm trickle of blood would begin to seep out and drip down my arm.

It was as though the blood that seeped out carried the pain with it. From my heart the hurt would flow through my arm and then out of the opening, allowing me to breathe again.
As soon as I saw that blood, I felt immediate relief from the ache that so often overwhelmed me.

I shook away the tears from my eyes as I stood up to make my way home-our time was up. After a momentary pause and a contemplative expression on her face, she asked,

"Can I give you a hug?"

The question shocked me, but not in a bad way, and I nodded my head yes.
She wrapped me into a light embrace and the tears I tried to shake off began to well up inside of me again. Her compassion towards me was overwhelming and unfamiliar to me.
I pulled away, wiping my eyes, and I walked out the door.

"How was it?"

my mom asked me as I stepped into the car.

"Good."

Offering my usual response of one or two words, I stared out the window and I felt warm. I felt like things were okay for that moment, and I wished that that moment would last forever.
I had this subtle feeling of hope creep up inside of me, like maybe I would finally get better.

***

Nestled just behind the quaint suburban neighborhood of uniform houses that we lived in there lay a vast outstretch of rolling hills.
Much like when I was a kid, I would often feel the pull towards the open space and would wander around back there, exploring the abandoned structures and finding myself in awe of the looming forest trees.
My life in the real world was painful and small, but out there I felt free.

On a chilly Fall afternoon, plugging in the headphones to my iPod, I made my way back into the hills to go for one of my regular walks.

Kicking up dust and pebbles with every step I took a deep breath of the clean open air and felt the rush of serenity washing over me again.
I ducked underneath the barbed wire fence that separated the narrow path from the outstretched land and made my way along to explore the unchartered territory. Along the way I would stop and examine old, rusted cans that lay on the ground, transformed into a deep, muddy maroon color by both the hands of time and mother nature.
I wondered where they came from, how long they had been there, how they had come to rest there.

There was a small structure whose original purpose was unclear that had been there for who knows how long, half standing and half sagging on the hill. I stepped up onto the unstable frame of the building and used a stick I had found along the way to poke at various things that were on the ground.
There was one thing that caught my eye in particular-it was a rusted old tricycle.
It was creepy and fascinating and took my mind towards any given horror movie that takes place in the hills.
After poking at it some, my interest eventually faded and I continued further into the hills, farther still than I had dared to venture before.
My oldest brother had at one point told me about a place that he had come across back there, that he called the "Pet Cemetery." I decided on this day that I wanted to try and find it.

As I paced about and searched for this place, I began noticing several bones lying about. A frigid wind lifted the corners of my shirt and sent a chill up my spine. The further I went, the more bones I would see, thigh bones, pieces of rib cages, a vertebra here and there. And there was something else, too. Dotted across the hills I saw these huge piles of sticks everywhere. They were roughly the size of a two-seated couch, artfully arranged, hundreds of them, all over.

I felt a queasy feeling in my stomach as I observed my surroundings and, despite feeling an overwhelming sensation that I should turn around and go home, I kept on walking. I was drawn to the inexplicably horrific scene that was hidden there.

Eventually I got to a sight that stopped me dead in my tracks and made my skin itch.

There was a small gulley tucked in where two hillsides came to meet, and there were a massive number of bones laying around, among them there were four cow carcasses, rather mutilated and torn apart, all side by side in the same small area.

I stood there in front of them, just staring, for quite some time.

I got as close as my courage would allow me to try and examine the dead animals. It was so peculiar that I felt for a second that I might be in a dream.

I couldn't help but noticed the way the sounds of the world fell away as I stood there, and it felt as though I were in a fishbowl.

I thought to myself how it was strange that I couldn't smell the decaying creatures.

All I could hear was my breath in my ears as the wind slowed and the hills grew silent.
Glancing around, I noted to myself the sheer number of bones that surrounded me. I counted all the different spines, keeping a tally in my head of how many cows-or other animals-had all come to pass here.
After some time, I felt I could not continue to exist there and that I needed to get home immediately. The wind howled again, and I noticed dark clouds creeping closer as the temperature began to drop.

"Storm's moving in,"

I thought to myself.

4

Summer rolled through and faded into early Autumn as my brothers and myself returned to school.
Well.... they returned to school, and I was dropped off there every day, only to ditch and find myself at the mall

smoking weed and cigarettes in hopes of scoring some alcohol or something better.
I would get out of her car, walk in the front doors of the building, shuffle through the hallways, dodging other students and avoiding eye contact, and walk out a side or back door somewhere, immediately leaving the premises and taking the bus to the mall or anywhere else but there.
It is not that I did not like school-I loved to learn and I was good at it, when I cared enough to try.
It was just that past experiences had taught me that people were bad and dreadful things happened to me when I went to school.
So, I simply made the decision to not go anymore. I felt at that point that any school was not somewhere that I belonged.

That day, the court room was near-silent aside from some muffled whispering of other patrons and the occasional cough or sneeze. I shifted my position, struggling to get comfortable on the hard wooden bench. Glancing at my mom, I could sense her disappointment in having to sit there with me once again.
I stood up when I heard my name called, and I made my way to the podium to stand before the judge. He looked to be in his fifties, not as clean cut as you would expect a judge to be. He had that fatigued look that only someone in his position could understand.
He quietly rifled through the papers in front of him as he glanced over my history and my record, occasionally looking up at me to give me the old' once-over. After an excruciatingly extended period of silence, he paused

what he was doing and asked me, quite frankly, the big question.

"Young lady, why aren't you going to school?"

Without hesitation, I looked him square in the eye and I told him that I hated it there. I explained that I had no friends, and that I felt I did not fit in there.
Somewhere along the way I had heard from one person or another about an alternative high school in the area and from the information I had gathered, I had reached the conclusion that I wanted to go there.
I asked the judge to put me in that school and to my surprise and with only a moment of consideration, he agreed. He went on to explain that he had sent some kids there before and he thought highly of the school and of the people who ran it.

I was enrolled within a few days.

***

Later that year, my best friend and I were hanging out in her room as we often did, waiting for the guys to pick us up and take us to the party of the weekend. Her at her desk, browsing on the computer and myself on the floor, staring up at the ceiling, taking life in one breath at a time as the drugs started to kick in.

My head was spinning, I closed my eyes and smiled as the rush of the music and the drugs mixed gloriously together and carried me away.

We talked and laughed and perfected our hair and makeup while we waited. I always found myself somewhere between adoration and jealousy when I looked at her. She was so perfect, so beautiful, fun, and outgoing.
Growing up with two brothers I never had the slightest idea of how to be a girl, but she took me in and taught me how to dress, how to style my hair, how to do my makeup in more flattering ways than the thick black eyeliner I had previously adopted. She was the sister I never had and had always wanted.
We were inseparable, regardless of how much our parents disapproved of us hanging out.
When the boys finally arrived, we rushed out the door past her already drunk father and we piled into their car. We knew one of them from somewhere but the other two were unfamiliar.
Not that hanging out with strange boys that were much older than me ever scared me off.

There were more of us than could comfortably fit in the small two door sports car, so we sat on the boys' laps in the back seat as we sped off down the street, taking swigs out of a small bottle of rum and attempting introductions over the loud music.
I felt so alive, the high from the drugs we had taken before they arrived was reaching its peak, the music blaring too loud to hear each other speak or to hear our

own thoughts as the driver showed off what his car could do.

We were doing about 113 mph down the interstate, and I felt a wave of fear and excitement rush through my veins for a moment, followed by this entirely liberating feeling of not really caring whether we lived or died.

Racing with another guy that the driver of our car was friends with, we flew down the highway headed for the same destination. The guy in the other car had a device that was able to detect if you were being radared by a police officer. He called us to let us know that they had clocked us going 115 mph.

In that moment, the sounds of the music and the shouting in the car faded away, and I wondered what my family was doing just then. I thought about if the car crashed, and I died, if they would be better off. I felt strongly that I would be.

We maintained our speed down the road and made a quick get-away off an exit shortly before our destination. They brought us to the top of a parking garage where we all got out of the car to wait out the police who would undoubtedly be looking for us.

Finding a suitable hiding spot at the very top of the garage, we hung out there for a while, taking swigs out of the bottle and popping some more pills that the guys had brought. My best friend and I kicked off our shoes and started to dance under the stars, not a care in the world. The night air was breezy and chilled as the sun-soaked pavement warmed our bare feet.

The alcohol often got me out of my head and out of my shell, and I depended on it for any social interaction.

When I was drunk and high, I became that other person that I always longed to be-happy, fun, and outgoing. It allowed me to be comfortable in my skin, like I could breathe again.
Compared to other times, when I was sober, my skin was two sizes too small, suffocating me.

On this night, I was alive, and I was free.

When we felt that it was safe to return to the streets, we made our way down from our hide out, and the rest of the night was spent in an apartment riding the high of the pills and drinking much more than we should have. In those moments, the rest of the world just fades away, there is nothing but the present, only the people you are with, and we are convinced that life will always be this way. We will be young, free, uninhibited, and released from the burden of all real or imagined responsibility. In those moments we cannot see where the road we are traveling down is going and we never have the slightest clue that where it is leading is a life filled with darkness and misery.

Perhaps we didn't know, or maybe we didn't care.

***

My first couple of years of high school seemed to pass me by in a blur of alcohol, drugs, partying. There was

rarely ever a day that went by that I did not find myself intoxicated on one substance or another.
I had found a small group of friends I fit in with, and they just so happened to drink and party like I did.
Surrounding myself with them made me feel less of a need to examine my own behavior.

Often, rather than being in class, we would find ourselves down the street at a friend's house smoking weed, or laying in the grass at the park nearby, passing around a bottle one of us had managed to get our hands on.
We would look up at the clouds, chain smoking one cigarette after another, taking hits of the weed every so often, talking and laughing.
Anytime we could get our hands on a bottle or a case of beer, we would surely drink it.
I am certain that most of the teachers in the school knew what we were up to, we were never quite as conspicuous as we liked to think we were.
Despite our ingenious attempts to hide the vodka in a Gatorade bottle or something of the sort, God knows we all stunk of it.
I suppose the teachers felt that getting us into more trouble would do no good. That's what landed us in that school in the first place-trouble.

There was one teacher though, the Dean of students, who took a particular interest in me.
He was a large man, standing around six'4, with a big, bald, tattooed head, tattooed arms and legs, and a rough, scruffy look. He was the kind of guy you would not want to find yourself on the bad side of.

My classmates would often talk about him, how at one point or another he had cussed them out or yelled at them about something.
He was no bullshit-and he would tell you like it was, regardless of whether it would hurt your feelings.
The students would gossip about how he used to be in a gang and how much time he had spent in prison, only to turn his life around and begin working for the very District Attorney that put him there-that DA was now the principal of the high school.

So, for whatever reason, this large, intimidating man took a liking to me. Or, rather, he seemed to believe in me.
I could not ever imagine why.

Every day, as I walked into school and walked by his desk, he would ask me to write down one thing that I liked about myself on a piece of paper.

"Any little thing, doesn't matter."

He told me.

It did not matter if it was something I had written before, or if it was something that seemed small and insignificant.
I would write this one thing on a torn off scrap of notebook paper and I would fold it up real small and I would give it to him.
Like a homework assignment.
There were many days when I would find that I could not think of anything that I liked about myself.

"This is stupid."

I told him.

"Come on, you can think of something. It can be physical, or it can be something in your personality."

He would not accept my attempts to forfeit.

Regardless of how I felt about the task, I humored him. He and I never had much real conversation, aside from the "things I like about me" moments, and the occasional small talk or questions about how my schoolwork was going.
Half the time I did not believe the things that I wrote down. I would stare blankly at the words on the piece of paper, knowing them in my head but completely failing to feel them in my heart.
I usually wavered between a sense of self-loathing or general apathy.

***

There was a moment at the beginning of my junior year in high school where I suddenly realized that all my friends there were a year older than me, and they would be graduating at the end of the year.
As if by fate or the will of the universe this sudden epiphany kicked me into full gear and I came to the decision that I did not want to be there without them, therefore I would graduate too.
Now, at this point I was about a year behind in terms of how much work I had done, so graduating a year early would mean needing to complete about 2 years' worth of work in 9 months. One thing I have come to understand about myself is that my stubborn nature can work either against me or in my favor, depending on what it is that I am dead set on accomplishing. Most times I have used my drive to self-destruct, but this time I used it for good.
My mom would often say to me,

"If you used half the amount of energy that you spend pursuing things that are bad for you, and instead put it towards something positive, you could do amazing things."

I wonder why I never believed her; I was so convinced that my life was never meant to be anything good.

Those 9 months went by in a blur of homework, stress, fear, and sheer determination; no matter what, I would not give up.
I was taking classes over winter break and spring break to earn all the necessary credits that I needed to walk on graduation day.
When I requested to take a class over winter break, my teacher agreed and, handing me the stack of homework assignments and readings that I needed, she eyed me with a mix of intrigue and doubt.
To complete the course, I would need to read two novels and write a literary analysis essay on each one. I could sense that she did not believe that I could do it, but I knew myself better than that.

That first day back from winter break. I waltzed into that school with my head held high and marched right up to that teacher, handing her the completed assignments. She looked through the two essays, leafing through each page in astonishment.

"Wow, Sarah. I am impressed."

The praise felt good.
I had done it; I completed an entire class by myself over a 2-week break. I was on top of the world, and it felt as though nothing could keep me from what I wanted to achieve.

The last couple of weeks of the year was a whirl wind of emotion. I scrambled around desperately trying to make sure that I had all the necessary credits. There were so many moments of doubt and uncertainty, where I was not sure if I would make it and the entire year, and all the challenging work felt wasted.

No matter what though, I refused to give in, I would wipe my face of tears and sweat and push on.

Against all odds I managed to squeeze out of high school an entire year early, at the age of sixteen.

A couple of weeks away from graduation, the Dean pulled me aside.
He handed me an old shoebox.

"A graduation present."

He fumbled over some words as he attempted to express how proud he was of me. Despite his inability to express himself, the thought alone that he would try stirred something inside of me. It was so unfamiliar, painful, and beautiful, to have someone care about me and believe in me like this.
I thanked him, and as he walked out of the classroom, I opened the box with peaked curiosity.
Piled inside the cardboard walls was every single neatly folded piece of paper that I had ever given him.
All those things that I liked about myself.
He had kept them all.

It felt as though all those times that I screwed up, everything that had gone awry were leading me up to this moment of triumph.
Maybe I wasn't a complete and total failure, after all.

***

5

As the excitement of graduation inevitably died down, I spent the summer waiting for my life to begin. It seemed that some of the clutter within my psyche shifted, and with it, my world turned upside down.

It's funny how you can just be moving along, living your life, and in the most unforgiving of moments, nothing would ever be the same.

In any given instant, everything can change.

The alarm clock next to my bed was lit with glowing red numbers, revealing the time of around 8:30 PM.
I was winding down for the night.
Without the slightest warning, I felt a deep wave of fear crash over me. A sensation that I can only describe as impending doom flooded every cell in my body. It hit me like a train, and it swept me away, taking my breath and my sanity along with its departure.
I had no idea what was going on, it was unlike anything I had felt before. I tried to force it out of my thoughts in hopes that the feeling would cease but it lingered on like a monster lurking in the corners of the room.
Freeing myself from the covers, I climbed out of bed, and made my way downstairs as genuine concern began to creep in. The world around me seemed as though it

were made of cheap plastic, everything became surreal, the way it feels in a dream-and this one had gone horribly wrong.

I felt that the possibility that I was losing my mind was very real.

I found my mom in the living room, and I pleaded with her to understand that something was wrong, and that I was scared. The sensation I was feeling was so obscure and I had nothing to compare it to, so I was largely unable to effectively communicate what was happening. I stumbled over myself trying to find the words, but they would not come.

I wasn't even sure how my mom could have helped, I just needed someone to comfort me in that moment.

Not realizing or comprehending what it was that I was going through, she brushed it off and went to sleep, leaving me alone for the remainder of the night.

I spent most of the night staring blankly at whatever was on TV in utter despair, attempting to distract myself from what I was feeling until I became so exhausted that I finally passed out.

I awoke the next morning completely drained. I was thankful that it was over, though.

At least I thought it was over.

These-what I soon came to know as panic attacks-continued incessantly every night for the rest of the summer. Without fail as soon as the sun would start to dip below the mountains and the sky darkened as the night crept in- the attacks would begin. They would continue to hit me in surges and waves of terror until I was so sleep deprived my body would shut down, usually around 3 or 4 in the morning.

At a time in my life where I was supposed to be enjoying myself and celebrating my graduation and acceptance into college, there I was instead: helpless and afraid. I was so haunted by these demons in my head that who I was as a person began to fade from lack of sleep and emotional exhaustion.
I began to feel like a ghost, watching the world move around me.
I felt very much like I was living in a nightmare that I was unable to wake from. The paralyzing fear deepened, unrelenting.
I felt trapped.
I was a prisoner of my own mind.

I had no idea how to escape the hell I was stuck in, and I genuinely feared that it would never end, that I would either need to kill myself or be committed to an institution. I cried to my mother on numerous occasions, but she did not know how to help me, she couldn't understand what was going on beneath the surface. Empathizing with mental health issues was never her strong suit, and I couldn't blame her, for she had never dealt with anything like it in her own life.

Out of sheer desperation for relief, I inevitably discovered that alcohol provided me solace from the storm, and I began doing whatever I could to get my hands on a bottle of whatever at night.

My mom quickly caught on to my thievery and started hiding her alcohol in various locations in the house and garage. She had underestimated my desperation though, and I would sometimes spend hours searching for the bottle until I got my hands on it and was able to drink myself to sleep.

What else was I supposed to do? I could not keep going on that way-something had to give.

After what felt like the longest 3 months of my life, I gave in and decided the only option that I had left aside from suicide was to see a doctor and plead for some medicated relief. My mom agreed to take me to see my primary care physician.

I sat on the table across from the doctor explaining as best I could to her what it was that I was going through, while attempting to maintain some semblance of sanity. She nodded in recognition and after a brief conversation she calmly informed me that what I was experiencing was called a panic attack which, unlike an anxiety attack, happens for no known reason.

My body was releasing adrenaline and my mind was responding accordingly to the perceived threat. No amount of deep breathing or self-soothing talk would change what was happening when I was caught in the thick of it. Once it had begun, I could do nothing more than ride it out.

She prescribed me a medication called Klonopin, which was a fast-acting tranquilizer that I was meant to take as soon as I felt the beginning of an attack coming on.

I could have cried tears of joy and relief, I finally had something that would help me. The nightmare was finally over. Or at least now I could sweep it under the bed and tuck it neatly away.

I was overwhelmed with gratitude for finally being offered some sort of solution.
At this point I had already developed the habit of drinking every night and while the medication that the doctor had prescribed did work for me, the alcohol and partying only worsened as I prepared to leave for college.

That first day of orientation had arrived, and my mom and I loaded her car up with all my belongings and made our way downtown so that I could move into the student housing apartments. I looked out the window and watched the world go by as I imagined how my life would be as a college student. I was so excited; I felt the possibilities of who I was and could be expanding with every mile that stretched between myself and my old life.
This moment was everything I had ever longed for-true independence and freedom.
We arrived at the student housing apartments and began unloading the car and bringing my things up to the room. We made pleasantries with the other parents and students as we passed by them in the hall. I felt as though I was floating on a cloud the whole time.
It truly felt like the first day of the rest of my life.

And yet…

If I were quiet enough, I could hear the cracks forming at the corners of my mind. I did my best to hold them together, to keep it from falling apart.
My hands would slip as my grip slowly weakened.

I feared that if I let go; if I let it break…
it would never be put back together again.

***

Though I felt that I was mature and grown up being on my own and in college, the reality was that I was barely 17 and I still had braces. I even had to ask the people around me at school to buy me cigarettes, for I was still too young to buy them myself.
The panic attacks continued nightly but at this point I was armed with my medication that I was instructed to take whenever I felt one coming on.

Despite my early age and my general nervousness about meeting new people, my commitment to drink and party saw to it that I managed to get my hands on some alcohol every night.
I would show up at the door of someone's apartment, bottle in hand, in hopes that someone else would drink with me. Maybe drinking with others helped me justify the fact that I was drinking every single night. Or maybe I just didn't want to be drinking by myself, because I felt that if I crossed that line, that that would make me a real alcoholic.
Though I did sense that my alcohol consumption was somewhat abnormal-for when other people wanted a night off, I genuinely didn't understand why. Isn't that what college was supposed to be about-having fun?
I didn't understand that it was even possible to have fun any other way.

Every night I found myself drinking till I blacked out, and every morning I would wake to growing feelings of shame and remorse, trying to piece together my actions of the night before.

I attended class less and less as the semester went on, I was simply too hungover for that. It was as if all my resolve and hope for a better life and a brighter future for myself had dissipated and my only interests involved alcohol, drugs, and securing my sense of self-worth through the attention of men.

It was sometime around noon as I awoke in a haze of confusion after one of my total black out nights. Accusatory rays of sunlight broke through the curtains and fell upon my face.
Groaning and squinting against the blinding light, I managed to roll myself out of my dorm bed and made my way to the restroom. Sitting on the toilet I held my head in my hands; my head was pounding. I felt awful. Suddenly I had the distinct feeling, or rather *knowing* that I had had sex the night before. I racked my brain for answers, desperately trying to find some sort of hint as to what had happened the night before.
I only knew one thing for sure, I had sex.

How could I not remember this? With whom?

Despite my attempts to force the memories of the night before, these questions drew up a complete and total blank.
I scrolled desperately through my phone in hopes there would be a clue in there. I texted a guy that I had been

talking to the night before and asked him what had happened.

"You really don't remember anything?"

he replied.

After pressing him, he confirmed my suspicions, that we had slept together.
The realization that I had slept with a guy who I had no intentions of sleeping with and had no memory of it whatsoever felt like a slap to the face.

The road I was traveling on suddenly seemed very grim and I knew that it was time for me to go home. The party was over.
At this point I had already dropped most of my classes so dropping out entirely wasn't that far of a stretch. I had been a failure so many times before but the sharp knife of letting my family down was never any less painful.

Feeling sick to my stomach about myself and the mess that had become my life, I picked up my phone and called my mom up. Her disappointment was obvious, but she did not ask many questions and agreed to come pick me up and help me move out. I think she could sense my desperation to get out of there.

It was late afternoon and the overcast, early October sun gleamed through the window, giving the room a soft yellow glow.
I was with some friends in the rec room of the student housing complex, and I stood in the corner, leaning against the wall as I gazed out the window, only half listening to their conversation as they played pool. I watched for my mom's car.

I just wanted to get out of there. I was so ashamed I could hardly look myself in the mirror anymore. Tears stung my eyes, and hard as I tried to hold them back, they nevertheless broke the barrier of my eyelids and softly rolled down my cheeks.
One of the guys in the room noticed me crying quietly. He walked over to me and without asking any questions, wrapped me in an embrace of pure compassion.
He held me in his arms as I cried, and there were no words between us. He saw a broken woman crying in front of him and somewhere inside his heart he felt the need to comfort me.

I was grateful for his lack of judgement.
I was grateful for the lack of questions, for I had nothing left to say.

I packed all my belongings into my mom's car that day, and the drive home was silent. I gazed at the building in the rearview mirror, ready to leave it all behind me.

My family didn't speak much about me dropping out, and the silence surrounding the subject made me sick

with shame. It felt like I was the family embarrassment for only lasting 2 months in college.
The holidays were the worst, seeing my aunts and uncles who would all inquire about how I was doing, and I would be forced to explain to each of them over and over that I was “taking a break” from school.

I hated that I had to admit my failures to everyone. I wished they would stop asking.
I wished that it had never happened at all, that I had never gone in the first place.

I kicked myself for having any sort of hope for the future, I should have known I was going to mess it up.

***

Tonight, I feel the weight of all the love that I have lost.
Of all the love that I will lose.
I am reminded,
Of the impermanence of everything.
Of the falling leaves and barren trees and the way the stars move across the sky,
the way that every cloud that passes over me will never look or move the same way again.
I feel the sorrow of the trees, as they stand in place much longer than I,
and they watch the world around them turn to dust.
And I feel their pain,
and their joy, their gratitude.
And I strive to be more like them.
As I, myself, grow, and my limbs extend like branches and my skin grows weary
and tired eyes take in the changing world around me.
And I pray to be more patient,
to be more present.
to be more hollow,
as I allow the things I love to slip through my fingers,
and I learn that nothing belongs to me.

And nothing ever stays the same.

***

6

You would think that doing heroin for the first time would be a significant moment in your life, but that was not the case for me.
There was no build up, no big fuss.
The first time that I tried heroin was surprisingly anticlimactic. It never seemed to be this big scary thing that you would think, it was just another way to escape from reality for me.
The consequences of this new venture failed to cross my mind whatsoever.
I was ignorant, and I had no idea what I was getting myself into.

I stood in the kitchen, leaning against the counter of a friend's house on a seasonably warm spring day, scrolling through the contacts in my phone. After trying and failing to find some pain pills that day on my own, I had made my way to his house to seek his assistance in scoring.

After leaving college I had enough sense scared into me by what had happened that I wasn't drinking as much anymore. I would still go to the occasional party, sure, but it was no longer a nightly venture. I had seen enough alcoholism in my family to recognize the path that I was going down.
Of course, since I was no longer drinking myself into oblivion every night, I desperately sought out other means to change the way that I felt.
We weren't having any luck with the pills, and, feeling frustrated with defeat, I was just about ready to give up and go home when my friend made me an offer.

"Why don't you try this instead?"

I looked up at him as he reached into his pocket.

Pulling his hand out, he produced a small, shiny black bag, roughly the size of a grape.

"What is it?"

I asked. Curiosity gripped me.

"Heroin."

The word fell out of his mouth casually, almost as though he weren't speaking about a deadly, highly addictive drug. However, at this point I cared so little for my life and well-being that it took next to nothing to convince me to try it. There was no hesitation, no, "maybe I shouldn't."

He went on to explain how much cheaper, stronger, and easier to find it was.
We sat down on the couch in the living room and, holding the bag between his thumb and forefinger, he tapped the light brown powder out of the bag and onto a piece of foil.

"Gunpowder."

He called it.

It had a smell like vinegar and a bitter taste to match.

We took turns smoking it off the foil, holding the cut piece of straw between our teeth as we followed the melted molasses looking substance as it slid down the aluminum foil, catching the smoke in our lungs as it rose.
The high was incredible. I almost immediately threw up, and I felt even better afterwards.
There was no fear, doubt, or regret. There was only this feeling like I had finally found what I was looking for. Heroin was like floating on a cloud, one where worry, stress, and fear simply don't exist. All your cares just melted away and for those hours or moments or however long, everything was just okay.

I was hooked. I would have given anything for that feeling of bliss, of nothingness, and over the next several years that is exactly what I did- I gave everything away.

Heroin doesn't care where you come from or where you're going, it will take everything from you, and, almost instantaneously, you will be too far gone to even try to stop it.

***

The decent into the void was less of an abrupt fall and more of a silent, sneaking spiral. It was as though I had no awareness that I was ever falling, as if one day I simply woke up at the bottom, wondering how I got there, struggling to put the shattered pieces of myself and my life back together.

The first time I felt physical withdrawals from heroin, I thought that I had the flu.

I was so clueless to the consequences of my actions, I failed to recognize them even when they smacked me right in the face.

After feeling strangely sick for a few days, bones aching, feeling run down and crappy, I recalled a friend of mine talking about being dope sick, and the realization suddenly hit me that that's what was happening to me.

This realization in hand, I wasn't sure how to feel.

There was a distinct sensation deep within me that told me that this meant that I had officially gone too far, and to never go back to it, but there was this other part of me that was largely indifferent, and that swiftly and easily convinced the greater part of myself that if I was able to get through it this time so easily, then maybe it wasn't so bad after all.

My mom eyed with me with suspicion as I lied and told her it must be the flu. She was always so keen on my behavior; she never failed to sense when something was up. I am certain that she never would have guessed what her daughter had gotten wrapped up in this time.

After several days of mulling about the house, mostly glued to the couch and flipping through the TV channels, I was feeling back to my old self.
Almost immediately following the relief of the symptoms, the memories of the sickness slipped away from my mind, and it was pushed to the far reaches of my psyche.
As those memories dissipated, the memories of how good the drug felt crept in to take their place, as well as the nagging, incessant boredom, and emptiness that I often encountered-the very feeling that I was always trying to escape.
I decided to call my friend that I had been picking up with recently, to see if he wanted to get high.

"Sure, pick me up in an hour?"

"Cool, I'll see you soon."

Hanging up the phone, my heart stuttered with a twinge of excitement, and I let out a sigh of great relief, knowing that I was going to be getting high again, knowing that I wouldn't have to sit in this simple existence any longer.

Some days it felt that my purpose was the drug, and that I existed for it. I lived and breathed to get high, to escape.
My skin always felt too tight, the room too small, and the air lacked whatever sustenance it was that I needed to feel at ease.

Drugs and alcohol, however, were the only thing that ever made me feel okay.
I did this dance with heroin for quite some time, until my slow and steady spiral turned into a sudden, sharp drop off into darkness.

***

7

Inevitably, my friends and I reached a point where smoking the heroin wasn't quite doing the trick anymore. The familiar ease and comfort that came from getting high was dull, far away, and I needed more of it to achieve the same relief.

Needing more drugs meant needing more money, and money was becoming more difficult to come by, especially when I couldn't hold a job for very long.

I had always been creeped out by needles, the thought of pushing something into my veins made my skin crawl. It used to be on my list of things I would never do. I had always had this idea that if I was just smoking it, I was still okay.
If I wasn't crossing *that* line, I was okay.

At least I'm not as bad as them, right?

Yet there finally came a day, where I found myself willing to do just that. I crossed each line that I drew for myself and pushed my boundaries out further, until there weren't any boundaries or lines left at all.

I pulled up to my friend's apartment, switching the ignition off and hopping out of the car eagerly.
I was coming from a doctor's appointment, where I had just been kicked out of the suboxone program for repeatedly failing UA's, so, naturally, my mindset was on full "fuck it" mode.
All I cared about was getting high. If they weren't going to help me, what was the point in even trying to be sober?
I latched on to this justification quickly.
Bounding up the stairs to the second floor, I knocked on her door in a rhythmic pattern, our way of signaling that it was a friend who inquired, and not the police or some other unwanted company.

"It's me."

I called through the door for added measure.

There was a pause, a quiet shuffling of bodies inside. I heard a click as the latch turned and the door unlocked, I quickly slipped inside and shut and locked the door behind me.

"Hey."

I greeted my friends, immediately finding my gaze drawn to the drugs on the table, I could feel my blood pressure rising with anticipation.
Two of my friends were already there.

The friend who lived there I had known for several years from the high school party scene. It seemed there were many of us who ended up entangled with the harder drugs.
She had a nice apartment near the city-her dad was a lawyer-and he had agreed to pay for the place so long as she was going to school.
Whether or not she ever actually completed any schoolwork, I was doubtful.

I handed her the small amount of money that I had, and she handed me a small bag of coke, and a small bag of heroin in exchange.
We had talked on the phone ahead of time, and she knew that I wanted to try the needle for the first time-she had already been shooting up for a few months.

Funny, I had tried on numerous occasions to convince her to stop shooting up, worried about her safety. Yet here I was, having swiftly forgotten any fear that I had about it in the first place.

I always seemed much more concerned with the well-being of my friends than I ever was for myself.

"Can you do it for me?"

Nervously, I asked her to help me.

"Yeah, of course."

She agreed.

I watched with peaked curiosity as she ritualistically laid out each of the supplies in front of herself on the table. She carefully broke off a small amount of each of the drugs into the small metal container and used a blue plastic water dropper to measure out several drops of water to mix it with.
She mixed the drugs in with the water and dropped a tiny cotton ball into the liquid.
Slowly and methodically, she uncapped the needle, and stuck the tip into the cotton ball, pulling back on the plunger and sucking the liquid up into the syringe.

"Wrap that around your arm."

She instructed me, pointing to the blue tourniquet that was laying on the table. I obliged, pulling the rubber

band tightly around my bicep and squeezing my fist. I watched as my veins began to bulge.
I observed with interest and a tiny bit of fear as she proceeded to stick the needle in my arm, finding a vein, and pushing the drug into my bloodstream.

I almost expected that I would be able to feel the drug go in, but the poison entering my bloodstream was relatively sensationless.

What I did feel is when the drug hit me.

Like a wave it proceeded to wash over my entire body, relaxing, rushing, pushing, and pulling.
I could smell the scent of the drug in my nose and taste it on my tongue as it enveloped me.

"Good?"

She asked me.

There was a twinge of concern as she studied my face, making sure she hadn't given me too much.

A smile crept across my face, and I silently nodded my head yes.
It wasn't nearly as scary as I thought it was going to be.
Closing my eyes, I let the feeling take over.

I was in love with it.

In love with the drugs, with the life, with the ability to forget about everything, everyone, including myself, for as long as I maintained the high.

I told myself I would chase this feeling forever.

***

I looked over at my friend as she sat in the passenger seat, unconscious. My mind raced, heart pounding in my ears and adrenaline flowing through my veins. Time slowed to a crawl, the world around us stopped and all I could hear was my own breath and the horrible gurgling, gasping noises that were escaping her mouth.

I snapped myself out of the stuck moment of terror, and I snapped into action, I sensed that I needed to act fast, or she was going to die.
Desperately, I grabbed the ice water that was in the cupholder, and I dumped it on her head, hoping the cold would wake her…no change.
Pausing, I frantically glanced around outside the car, surveying our surroundings in fear that someone would see what was going on and call the police.

We were alone in the parking lot; it was late at night in the small town we were in.
Feeling assured that we were alone, I climbed on top of her and began pushing against her chest and slapping her in the face, calling her name over and over, blowing air into her mouth.
I begged her to wake up.
Her only response was a continuation of the awful noises she was producing as she unconsciously struggled to breathe.
I had no idea how to do CPR, or if any of this was what you were supposed to do in an overdose. No one teaches you these things, there is no handbook on how to save someone's life and not a single one of us ever grows up thinking that this is something we would need to prepare ourselves for.

I didn't dream of being a junkie when I got older, I never wanted this. Quite simply I had no idea what I was signing up for when I took those first hits of heroin. I was a fool then, and now it was too late.
After about 30 minutes or so of attempting to wake my friend, I was having no luck, so I just sat there and began to cry.

What do I do? Where do I go?

I just wanted to be a kid again, I wanted to go back in time and fix this.
I thought about that first time I did heroin, and I cursed the old me for being so stupid.
I knew in my gut it was time to take her to the ER, or she was going to die right there next to me. I started the

car and followed my GPS to the first ER that I could find.
I walked into the doors, I wasn't calm, but I'm sure I was too high to appear frantic. I was terrified of the repercussions of this, but I could not let her die.
I quickly found the lady at the front desk.

"Hi, I, uh, my friend is in the car, she's not breathing. I think she took some drugs."

I stumbled over my lies as she eyed me with suspicion.

I wondered how many times she had watched a scene just like this unfold. Her non-reaction told me that it was not the first time.

Tiny beads of sweat formed across my hairline as I stumbled over my words trying to tell these women what was going on. I could feel their judgement and disgust as they blinked at me in silence.

"Okay, where is the car?"

They asked me.

I led them out the front doors and to the car where my friend sat unconscious. After seeing her in the flesh and recognizing the severity of the situation, they quickly sprang into action, picking her up and gently setting her down in a wheelchair.

Once she was secured in the chair, they burst into action, rushing her back into the hospital; there was no time to waste.
I watched, helpless as they took my friend away.

After following them inside, they stopped me to explain that I was not allowed in her room. It felt like a slap to the face as I realized that these people thought that I might be a danger to my friend.

Was I?

I placed their judgements upon my back, and I carried them with me for a long time.

I was in shock. I don't know if my brain could even comprehend what it was that had happened. I walked out of the hospital in a daze, and I got back in the car and sat in the parking lot for quite some time.
You would think that this experience would deter me from using, however it only made me want to get high even more; I couldn't bear the pain that I was feeling. I wished it were me that had overdosed.
I continued shooting cocaine and heroin into my veins in the parking lot of the hospital while I watched the sun come up. The car I was driving belonged to my friend, and I wasn't sure exactly what to do next. So, I just sat there, watching the world go by around me.
Always observing from behind that pane of glass, behind the walls that I had built around myself.

I watched as people walked their dogs, as they came into work in their scrubs, cups of coffee clutched in their hands as they hurried along.

They looked happy, content, satisfied with their lives. I wondered about each one, about what it was like to be normal. I thought about what errands they might be running that day, about where they lived and who they were as people, about their families and their hobbies. My heart was heavy as I felt that I was observing a life that I could simply never have. It just wasn't meant for me. It was like a complicated math equation that I just couldn't figure out. It was right there in front of me, but no matter how hard I tried, I failed to reach it. One way or another, I always fell short.

I could never figure out how to be "normal," how to not be a criminal and a junkie and a low life.

I thought about that story of how I was born, about how I used to believe the words my mother spoke when she called me her "miracle child." I thought about how that feeling had changed over the years and how those words became twisted into regret.

I felt that God had made a mistake in letting me into this world and now He was trying to take it back. I succumbed to this belief, and I did everything in my power to assist him in taking me back, often teetering on the fence between life and death.

Several hours later, after ignoring the phone calls that blew up my phone, I finally answered and told my friend's boyfriend what had happened, and he began grilling me with questions to piece together the night before. I answered them as best as I could, and we

agreed to meet some place so that I could hand off her car to him.
A brief time later, he pulled up next to me. He got into the car and my heart raced as I was filled with fear, shame, and remorse. I knew this was my fault, I would forever carry this with me.

There wasn't any insult he could throw at me that I hadn't already thrown at myself.
I braced myself for the screaming and cussing but he was surprisingly calm and gentle. We talked for some time, and I fell apart in tears, begging for forgiveness. I never intended for any of this to happen. I never wanted to hurt anyone, aside from myself.
I asked him how she was doing, and he told me she was stable, but had I waited any longer to take her in, she would be dead.

He looked at me, studying me as if trying to understand me, his eyes were filled with pity,

"Sarah, you need to get some help."

He was right, and it's not that I didn't want help, I just didn't know how. I no longer believed I was capable of being helped. Mostly, I was just patiently waiting to die.

We parted ways, and that was the last time I ever saw my friend. Everyone in our circle quickly found out what happened and one by one I was cursed and shunned. I accepted my fate as the outcast, for this was a familiar label for me.

I accepted the hate that they threw at me, I felt that I deserved it.
I hated me, too.

And I was alone again.

***

I kept my place on the tattered old couch in the small apartment, feeling rather small and childlike while this man stood above me, threatening to kill me and my family. The air smelled like stale cigarettes and old beer soaked deep into the carpet fibers.

I really messed up this time.

My stomach writhed itself into knots as I sat in partial disbelief of the situation that I had managed to find myself in. I tended to have this rather aloof air about me and never took anything so seriously, mostly because I had already faced so much trouble and danger that it didn't really phase me anymore.

This time, though, I was scared.

About a week prior to this moment, I found myself in a black out drunk at some random party-nothing new there.

I had been party-hopping at various houses in town and wound up in the very same apartment where, unbeknownst to me, my life would later be threatened.

I was in the bedroom with the guy who lived there-this was our first time meeting each other, and since he had the coke, of course I stuck with him for the evening.

He scared me, though.

I had been around plenty of shady people, but this guy had this subtle instability about him that put you on edge whenever you were around him, like he could just snap at any moment.

His head was shaved bald, and he had tattoos covering his arms.

We sat on his bed taking shots out of the bottle and snorting lines of blow while he ranted on about various things.

At one point someone else from the party began knocking on the door and, I guess he didn't like that because he jumped up off the bed abruptly, ripped open the drawer of his desk, and pulled out his gun. Stomping over to the door, he flung it open, pointing the gun directly at the guy's head,

"What the fuck do you want?"

he barked.

The guy, terrified, begged him to calm down and quickly retreated to the party, apologizing for the interruption.
I'm not sure what it was I felt in that moment, there was a slight queasy feeling in the pit of my stomach, like I knew somewhere inside that I was somewhere I shouldn't be, but I ignored it.
My safety and well-being were extremely low on my priority list.
If they were ever there at all.

Setting his gun on the edge of the bed, he turned back towards me as I was lighting a cigarette. Another party go-er would pop in from time to time at his discretion and join us in our private party. I always felt like a VIP for some reason, whenever I could hang out in the dealer's room or whoever had the drugs.
I had this massively distorted sense of what it meant to be cool, I guess.

At some point in the night, despite the display of violence and aggression I had seen from this man, and despite the sick feeling in my stomach, I had what I believed to be a clever idea. I believe that I went into it with the best of intentions, and maybe I even fooled myself with my lies.
Somehow, I convinced this dangerous, psychotic man to front me a quarter ounce of his cocaine, so that I could sell it for him. I always had a way with words, so convincing him was no feat. Hell, I even had myself convinced.

I had already recently been involved in some minor drug running and middle-man stuff, so it wasn't THAT far off to move a quarter ounce, right?
He thought my idea was as good as I did, and so that night I went home with the drugs.

I proceeded to fall through the next few days plowing through those bags of cocaine. I sold some of it, sure, but for the most part I managed to shoot up almost the entire quarter ounce of cocaine into my own veins within a matter of days.
I had no control. I knew the consequences I was faced with, and I still couldn't stop myself.
Sitting on the floor of my closet, I dug through the bags, holding each one up to the light to check for anymore that I could scrape out.

How was it already gone?

It seemed impossible.
The weight of the situation fell on me as the realization of what I had done set in.

Shit.

Now face to face with the consequences of my actions, I stared at my feet and the fibers of the carpet as he screamed at me, demanding an explanation for where his coke went and why I didn't have his money.
I lied, of course.
I told him my mom had found it and flushed it. That was believable, right?

No amount of talking was going to get me out of this one, though.

"I know where you live, I know where your family lives, my homegirl is going to beat your fucking face in if you don't get me my money."

I felt deep in my soul that his promises weren't empty.

"I'll get it, I will."

I begged for his patience and swore that I would get him his money, and it was the truth because I knew I had no choice.
I left his apartment that day, mind racing, trying to think of what I was going to do and how I would get the money. I practiced the conversation that I would have with my mom, and what I would say to explain to her why I needed several hundred dollars.

She's going to kill me.

She was used to my bullshit by now, but this was a new low for me.

I've always had this feeling that something was watching over me, and this situation was a perfect example of that.

Days went by and I didn't hear from him.
Days turned into weeks, and still no word.

It was only much later that I had found out that he had been arrested for some reason or another and gone to jail.
At this point I was a wreck, constantly looking over my shoulder and flinching at any movement or noise.
My life went on like this for the duration of my drug use, always looking over my shoulder and fearing for my life and freedom.

It was exhausting, and I often felt that I was barely hanging on.

***

I tried to get sober on numerous occasions, God knows I tried.
On one of these occasions, late in the Fall season, my mom and I put our heads together and came up with a plan. Her insurance never covered any behavioral health and so rehab was usually out of the question. We were desperate, though, and we both knew I needed more help than mere therapy could provide.

We sat on the stiff, upholstered chairs across the desk from the director of admissions at a rehab/sober living facility downtown. My attention drifted in and out as my mom discussed payment options since our insurance wouldn't cover anything there.
It felt sort of odd, sitting across from this person, talking about getting sober as I sat there, high as a kite. They would ask me questions like what I used, how much, how often, and how did I use it. I would answer, shamefully casting sideways glances at my mom who was clearly embarrassed for me, too.

I wondered if they could tell I was high right then.... probably.

I'm sure I wasn't the first person to come in here under the influence, whose mother was desperately trying to save them.

We came up with a plan that we all agreed upon, and so it was decided. I would once again try out this sober thing.
We stepped outside and the air was cool and crisp, yellow, and orange leaves decorated the sidewalks and scattered about the air as they fell from their branches.
I loved Fall.
I felt a tinge of excitement deep in my stomach as I realized that I was going to get to spend this holiday season sober. I would get to be fully present, as opposed to being numbed out and far away in the way that the drugs made me.

Maybe this would be all right.

The program that I was in had me spending 28 days of "inpatient" treatment within the homes. It was a collection of three houses that sat side by side from each other, one for men, one for women, and then there was the main house where we all attended groups and ate lunch and dinner and such.
It wasn't so bad there, I got fed decent food three times a day, and I sat in group all day with a collection of my peers. It felt nice being surrounded by people to whom I could relate. I listened as they described their experience with their own addictions, giving life to all the things that I never knew how to say.
Over the month we spent there, we grew quite familiar, learning each other's secrets and demons. Each of our individual darkness was dumped out on the tables for each other to see and we would help one another sort it out.

I spent Christmas in rehab that year. My family came to see me that day, they each brought me a present and we got to sit with each other in the lobby of the facility as they watched me open each one and they all expressed their gratitude that I was doing so well.
I was overjoyed. I never realized that life could be so beautiful, so full of love.
My mother's eyes welled up with tears as I told her about how I felt happy for the first time in longer than I could remember.

I felt guilty that I couldn't get anyone presents in return, but they assured me my sobriety and well-being was the best gift they could have ever received.
My heart swelled with gratitude.
Within that feeling lay an insidious, tiny sense of fear.
Fear that I would take their gift back, that I wouldn't be able to be the daughter that they needed.
Always, in the back of my mind, the fear that I would fail again.
I did not let them see this doubt within me, and I stuffed it away and shook it from my bones as I returned their smiles and relished the moment where my family was finally proud of me.

Once the 28 days of inpatient was up, that meant that I was able to get my car and my phone back, and I was required to leave the house every day looking for a job.
I felt so lost in the world, so out of sorts.

Where did people find jobs?

I was only 20 years old, and I had spent so much of my teenage years doing drugs and drinking, I felt like I had no idea how to function in the world.
Following guidance from the staff and other clients, I went to the library one day and used their computer to search for jobs on Craigslist.

I wasn't sure what I was supposed to do with a whole 8 hours. I didn't have any hobbies, I hadn't the slightest clue what I liked to do or what there even was to do aside from drink and use drugs. I was a fish out of water.

My discomfort in this new world grew and on the second day, a thought had quietly crept into my mind to call up an old friend.
I spent the remainder day driving around picking up everything I needed to shoot up, and then picking up drugs, in the same exact way that one might drive around to run errands.
I found myself sitting in my car and I looked at the set up in front of me, the loaded rig.
I felt a sharp pang of guilt as I thought about the 45 days I had of sobriety, about how happy my family was for me and my newfound life.
I sunk the needle into my skin and pushed down on the plunger and the guilt quickly washed away as the high rushed in to take its place.
It had been a while since I had gotten high, so my lower tolerance made it that much better. I felt relieved as the amber liquid flowed through my bloodstream and made my whole body feel warm.

It felt like coming home.

In a way, I was coming home. I was fleeing from the unfamiliar and the uncomfortable and all those things that I didn't know how to do in the real world, and I was rushing back to the familiar, settling into my old rut.
It was only about a week after that that I knew I would be caught eventually, and so I left "voluntarily," to avoid that whole scenario and the shame that failing a UA would bring.
My mom couldn't understand why I wanted to leave, and her confusion and disappointment ripped my heart out of my chest and crushed it.

"I'm sorry, mom."

I found myself repeating this over and over for weeks. She would often question me about what had happened, why I had left.
I think she knew, but she just wanted me to admit it.
It never took her long to know that I was using again. If she ever had any suspicions all she would have to do is say "show me your arms," and the argument was over. There was never much room to deny anything, just a lot of hollow apologies and a tangled web of shame that wrapped itself around and within me.

I couldn't stand myself after that, knowing that my mom had used part of her retirement money to get me help, and that I had thrown it all away.

The guilt and shame were this constant whispering in my ear, picking away at me and driving me back to the drugs, desperate to numb it all away.

The ultimate paradox of addiction-the behaviors of a drug addict brings about great shame and guilt, and so they return to the drugs repeatedly to rid themselves of these painful feelings.

To rid themselves of any semblance of a human being.

***

I frantically glanced down from the road to my phone, which had been ringing non-stop. This time it was my dad. My heart rate slowed a bit when I finally got across county lines as I sped down the interstate.
After ignoring the first few calls, I caved and decided to answer.

"Dad."

My voice cracked as I choked back tears.

"Sarah, what are you doing? The cops are looking for you. Where are you?"

His voice sounded calmer than I felt, and I was grateful for that. He asked me the question, but both him and I knew that I would never tell him. It was too late now.

"Dad, I fucked up, I don't know what to do."

The tears began to flow down my cheeks, and I quickly wiped them away. I knew I had made a huge mistake, and the pressure of the police calling my phone and asking to speak to me sent my head into a tailspin. My thoughts were racing.
If I turned myself in, my life would be over.
I was stuck in this life that felt as though it didn't belong to me.

"We'll get you a consult with a lawyer, don't talk to anyone,"

he told me,

"I'll help you."

Listening to him speak the words, I could hardly believe that my father was willing to help me clean up this mess and escape conviction. Then again, he always did try to protect me.

The more miles that I put between myself and that dusty old town the better I felt, I at least figured they wouldn't be looking for me two counties over.

For now, I was safe.

I pulled into a parking lot and dialed my dealer's number, letting him know that I had arrived and what kind of car I was in.

"5 minutes."

He told me, as he always did.

I sat there wondering how many hours of my life I had spent waiting on drugs, waiting on money, waiting for an end to the suffering.

I met with him and got what I needed, climbing back into the car, and I drove around the area looking for a good area to shoot up-one where I wouldn't be interrupted.

I took the tiny plastic knot in between my teeth and ripped the bag open, the smell of vinegar and burnt sugar filled my nose and I felt immediate relief of the withdrawals and anxiety that was driving me.

I broke off a small piece and cooked it down in the small metal tin, watching the amber liquid fill the plastic rig as I pulled back the plunger.

In that moment, what I had done to get here didn't even matter, I had my hands on my relief, on the one thing I felt I needed to survive, and so for the time being, I was okay.

I pressed the needle into my skin and gently pulled it back, finding a vein, and I pushed the drug into my bloodstream.

I took a deep breath and let the sensation wash over me as the withdrawals melted away.

I could taste the drug as it swarmed through my body, I could even smell it. This moment, this feeling, this reprieve, it controlled me. Day in and day out, I was a slave to my addiction.

Once the heroin set in and my mind was at ease, I was reminded of the stark reality of my situation. I picked up the phone and called my dad again, asking him what to do.

We agreed that I should stay at his house for a while, as the police had already begun showing up at my mom's house, looking for me.

I was driven by pure instinct and survival mode; I had little thought to consequences at this point. I did what my dad told me to, and after we made it safely back to his house he called and made an appointment with a lawyer for the following day.

My legs were shaky and nervous as I slunk into the lawyer's office, I felt so out of place. I stuck out like a sore thumb. I could always feel people's eyes on me when I was in a room like that, feel their judgements boring holes into my skin.
I let my gaze fall to its usual place-the floor-and avoided eye contact with everyone around me.
I could sense my dad's impatience as we sat waiting to speak with this man who would give us some insight into what my fate could be.
Eventually, they called us back.

I sat in the chair in a small, expressionless room across from a well-manicured, calm looking man in a suit. He asked me a lot of questions, wanting me to explain everything that had happened, from the beginning. As I spoke, I shifted my eyes between him and his hands as he jotted down notes, his face not giving the slightest idea into what he could have been thinking. It was unsettling, telling this well-rounded man who had likely never had so much as a parking ticket about all the crimes I had committed over the last 2 weeks. Although, he didn't seem taken aback by any of it.

After I finished telling my story, he called my father back into the room. I lowered my head as my dad walked in, feeling a great wave of shame wash over me. Here this man was, doing whatever he could to help his daughter.

I did not feel as though I deserved it.
The lawyer explained that if charged, I would likely be looking at about five different felonies, ranging from Class 5-Class 3. My stomach twisted as I listened to him explain the various charges that I could face, and the likely amount of prison time for each charge.
I knew that I had messed up, but the weight of the circumstances did not fully sink in until that moment. My mouth felt dry as I struggled to swallow down my fear.
Towards the end, though, he explained that if a warrant wasn't already out for my arrest, that they did not have enough evidence to charge me.
He advised that I avoid talking to those police that were calling my phone and leaving messages.

"If you talk to them, they will use their interrogation skills to get you to incriminate yourself, so don't do it."

He advised.

I nodded solemnly, struggling to take in what all of this meant for me.
I was grateful for his lack of judgement, and his advice. My dad and I walked out of his office in silence. There wasn't really anything left to say at that point. I was going to hide out at my dad's house for a while and take the lawyer's advice and not talk to the police. He gave us a website address where we could check every day to see if there had been any warrants issued.

So, each day we checked, and we waited.

***

9

The holidays were here again. I gazed at the bleak landscape that lay just outside my window, watching the pillowy white snow drift down, coming to its final rest upon the ground.

I had the vaguest sensation of memory of a time when the holidays made me happy, but it felt faded and just out of reach.

This year, as Christmas grew nearer my heart grew heavier. I knew that my mom and brothers and dad would all be going to my aunt or uncle's house, as we did every year. It was our family tradition.

I also knew that I was not welcome this year.

I certainly couldn't be angry about it; I had this tendency to steal from whoever I could whenever I had the chance to feed my drug habit.

I wouldn't want me in my house, either.

I sat in my room alone, listening to music and the muffled sounds of my mom and brothers getting ready to leave.

"You good?"

My oldest brother stuck his head in my room. I could see the hurt written all over his face, watching his sister slowly kill herself and his family get torn apart over it.

I felt sick with guilt again.

"Yeah, I'll be fine."

I lied.

Turning his eyes downward, he silently nodded and retreated downstairs.
He wasn't convinced.
My mom and I had gotten in an ugly screaming match that evening, and her accusations of "worthless" and "failure" echoed throughout my head.
She was right.
Hearing the hum of the garage door opening, I stood off my bed and watched out my window as the headlights pulled out of the driveway and disappeared into the night.
I was so hurt, but I would never admit it-to myself nor anyone else.

I don't need them.

I tried to tell myself.
I don't know if I thought that would make me feel better, but it didn't.
So, I did the only thing that I knew how to do- I went downstairs, opened the fridge, and made myself a drink from my mom's stash of booze.

Getting good and drunk, I spent the night flipping through the channels and slowly sinking deeper into the couch, and into my own head.

The alcohol helped, but there was still this nagging, incessant ache within my heart that I felt might tear me in two at any given moment.

Tears welled up in my eyes but would not fall. I thought I might scream; all this pain and I couldn't even let it out.

I couldn't take it anymore, and, sighing heavily with defeat, I went upstairs into my room and pulled the pair of haircutting scissors I kept in my makeup drawer out.

I sat on the edge of my bed, staring at the blade, running my finger along the edge.

"Please just let me die."

I begged whatever God there might be, but the only response was a room full of silence.

With swift and sure movements, I pushed the blade hard into my arm, and quickly swiped it to one side, feeling my skin rip open with a sharp sting.

The smallest bit of relief crept in, and I continued the motion; watching as the wound on my arm split wider, and blood began to seep out at the corners, the warm liquid dripping down my arm.

The more I bled, the better I felt, and the pain that I was feeling slowly faded away into the background.

I wanted more, more relief…just. More.

I slid the blade over the cut once more, when I was jolted out of my focus by a sudden burst of blood that shot out of my arm.

"Shit."

I gasped, quickly slapping my other hand over the wound to stop the blood from shooting out.

I frantically looked about the room, not knowing what to do. I ran into the bathroom, so that the blood would fall into the bathtub rather than on the carpet. It was dripping off my arm at an alarming rate.
I had accidentally hit a vein, and dread filled my stomach.
Was it an accident?

They're going to lock me up again.

I was officially panicking.

How was I going to explain this?

The blood was seeping out from under my hand, in between each finger, despite my efforts to put pressure on the wound. It was warm and thick.

God, what do I do?

I prayed again.

Remembering some medical show that I had seen at some point in the past, I raised my arm above my head to slow the bleeding.
I couldn't help but acknowledge the faintest realization that maybe I *didn't* want to die.
I sat on the edge of the tub and prayed. I promised that I wouldn't ever do this again if God would just make the bleeding stop.
To my surprise and great relief, after several minutes the blood began to coagulate and slow to a crawl.
Thanking the unseen force of the universe, I wiped the sweat from my forehead.
After a minute or so of catching my breath, I dried the remaining tears from my eyes and began to dig through the cabinets in the bathroom.
I collected some supplies to dress the wound. Wrapping my arm tightly, I paused and glanced around the bathroom, examining the scene.
Little beaded droplets and smears of blood decorated the floor and the bathtub.

Turning back to the sink, I soaked a washcloth in warm water and began to clean it up, hiding the evidence from when my family would get home.

***

I was completely out of control.
I often felt like a prisoner in that house, desperation and insanity controlled my every move like a marionette. My addiction was like a demon inside of me, raging in circles of destruction and despite my many futile attempts to get sober, repeatedly I proved to be completely and utterly powerless. Any fire of hope within me grew very dim; it was sometimes nothing more than a soft ember and a puff of grey smoke.
I was a slave, and heroin, my master.

Feeling my blood begin to boil I could sense the withdrawals were coming on quick. I had to get out of there, I had to get well. Every inch of my skin crawled, I was suffocating. When the withdrawals hit, any semblance of a human being in me ceased to exist. My morals and values and everything I cared about disappeared and I was nothing more than a rabid animal in survival mode, ready to take down whatever stood between myself and the drug.

My mom and I were fighting again. I could not understand why she wouldn't just let me be and she could not understand why I couldn't stay sober.
A friend of mine was on the way to pick me up, but he was taking forever, as usual.
I needed to get well. I couldn't think, I couldn't breathe. The screaming match my mom and I were engaged in was only amplified by the raw emotion of the withdrawals, and I was fuming. I became this fire raging out of control, a force of destruction.
I knocked my mom's plant off the ledge and felt only the tiniest sliver of guilt as I watched it crash to the ground. The pot shattered and clumps of dirt and aloe leaf were strewn across the floor.
I was in a black out now, I wanted to destroy everything, tear it all down. I wanted my surroundings to match the chaos that I felt inside of me.
I stood in the kitchen across from my mom. She looked at me in a way I will never forget-like she couldn't believe she had created such a monster. Neither of us recognized the person that I had become.

I was just like my father.

In a sudden explosive fit I kicked my foot backwards into the wall. The drywall gave way to the force of my foot, and my leg crashed right through it.
My mom had had enough, she couldn't stand by and watch me tear her house apart anymore and she picked up the phone and called the police to have them remove me from her home.

"Go ahead and call the police,"

I screamed at her,

"I don't fucking care."

I retreated to the garage to smoke a cigarette and catch my breath and shortly afterwards the police arrived. They entered the garage and stood in front of me, asking what had happened here. They had seen the damage to the walls and the house and I'm sure they expected someone a lot bigger and meaner looking than the 100-pound little girl that sat in front of them.

We talked for some time, and they explained to me that I had to leave as my mom did not want me there. I told them I was waiting for a ride, and I was more than willing to leave; I did not want to be there any more than she wanted me there.

My mom had entered the garage at this point and we both spoke with the police officers regarding my addiction. They told me that I had the option of going to detox if I wanted to.

My heart was split entirely in two. I wanted to be sober, I didn't want to live this way anymore-who would? Yet I felt that I was stuck; I did not know how to be sober. The withdrawals terrified me, the thought of never using again shook me.

I hated heroin, everything that it was, everything that it made me, but I was completely and hopelessly addicted to it.

"I don't want to go."

It was only half true.

The officers persistently attempted to convince me, along with my mother.
She was crying now.

"Please Sarah,"

She looked at me with tear-filled eyes.

The sight of her breaking heart ripped mine to pieces. Relief from the withdrawals was only a few blocks and a few minutes away. Every inch of my body screamed at me to leave and go get high. I looked up at my mom, I could feel the pain that I was causing her.
Tears began to stream down my face as I hung my head in defeat.

"Alright, I'll go."

The tears flowed down my mom's face in a rush of relief.

She wrapped me in a hug and thanked me repeatedly. I was so angry at myself for my decision, but I could not bear to break my mom's heart any longer. My love for her and her love for me was in that moment just strong enough to momentarily break the hold that heroin had over me.

After finishing detox, I was prescribed a drug called Suboxone-to help with the cravings-and I managed to stay off heroin for a couple of months. I had gotten a job, and things seemed to be heading in the right direction.

There was this constant nagging feeling of boredom and emptiness, though. It lingered within me, incessantly whispering in my ear that this life was not enough for me. I was relieved that my family wasn't worrying about me, but I did not feel an ounce of contentment in and of myself.

The hole that heroin's absence left within me desperately sought a replacement, so I began drinking heavily on a nightly basis again, very much like the way that I was before I had stumbled upon the insidious drug in the first place.

I could not stand what it was to be completely sober, the hollow feeling in my heart would pick away at me throughout the day until I could get home and get some drinks down to ease my sense of aching discomfort.

***

10

My 20th birthday had arrived, and all I wanted was to have a good time-which for me usually meant drinking and drugging my way into oblivion. A few of my friends were planning a small get together, and, after a long shift of eyeing the hands on the clock, I got out of work, and I made my way home to get ready for the night. Windows down, I stuck my hand out as I drove to feel the warm wind flowing over my skin.

At home, I poured myself a vodka and tonic and went up to my room to crank up the music. Trying on various outfits, I would discard the failed options on the floor, sifting through the remaining clothes in my closet.

Sipping my drink, I felt the warm sensation deep in my belly. The night had begun.
I texted my friend that I used to work with, to see if she knew where to find some coke. She quickly responded, suggesting that I meet her at the seedy little motel where she was working at the time.
Feeling a surge of excitement, I quickly finished my drink and the final additions to my makeup, and I rushed out the door.

"Going out."

I shouted to my mom as I closed the door behind me.

I swung my car into the parking lot, my palms began to sweat the way they always did when I was anticipating getting high. I hung out with her as she worked the front desk for some time, we talked and laughed, and I poured some of the pint that I brought with me in a glass and sipped it as we waited for one of the residents of the hotel to get back from his job-he was the one who had the drugs.

I found myself immediately sizing him up as he walked through the lobby of the hotel. He was middle aged, a large, rounded belly, relatively clean cut. Looking at him, you would never suspect the extracurricular activities that he was into. He just looked like a regular guy.
He worked for one of the oil companies that had taken up residence in our town when it was discovered that fracking held the potential for major profits.

He was a supervisor there and made a substantial amount of money, which helped him fund his drug addiction.

My friend explained to him the situation and he laughed and agreed to help me get what I was looking for. My stomach churned with anticipation as I followed this stranger into his hotel room and sat on one of the beds. I watched him pace about the room, kicking off his boots and gathering up his supplies as he made light conversation.

The hotel was small and dingy, a hideous sea green carpet decorated the floor, with heavy curtains covering the windows, pulled shut so that the room was dark. Glass ashtrays lay atop the counters, with half smoked cigarettes snubbed out inside of them.
I pulled one of my own out of my pack, placed it between my teeth and lit it, filling my lungs with the harsh smoke as I took a long drag.

"It's my birthday, so I'm just looking for some party favors."

I explained.

"Well, happy birthday!"

He flashed me a car-salesman-smile.

I thanked him, reaching into my purse, and producing my rig and supplies. I could feel my heart pounding in my chest, almost as if I were high already.

I glanced up at what he was doing, and I noticed that the drug he produced looked like a foggy shard of glass, as opposed to the white powder that I was expecting.

"Oh…that's not coke."

I said, obviously confused.

"No, this is speed."

I watched him crush the foggy crystal down into his tin and load up a shot.
There was next to no consideration for whether I should try this new drug. Almost immediately I convinced myself that, since I was there already, and it WAS my birthday, I might as well try it out.
He set his needle aside, and I watched with eagerness as he loaded up my shot.
I held the shot in my hand, looking down at the clear liquid inside the syringe.
I had never done this drug before, but it did not scare me. I just didn't know what to expect.
Quickly finding a vein, I pushed the drug into my blood stream.
My heart began to convulse, my stomach dropped, and I could smell the pungent odor of the drug as it coursed through my veins. A heat rose in my chest, and I coughed as the ether produced from the drug escaped my body.
The world slowed to a crawl, and everything around me began to dance in a slow waving motion.
I sat there, staring at the wall, stunned.

The effect of the drug was far more intense than I could have imagined, and after a couple of minutes I was forced to rush into the bathroom and vomit.
The initial wave of the drug crashed into me and made me feel sick.
I had never felt anything like it, it was incredible.
I returned to my place in the bed, the dazed expression remained on my face.

"You good?"

he inquired.

I laughed,

"Oh yeah."

I sat there for some time, taking it all in, and the man and I talked for a while. I told him about how I was sober off heroin, and he commended me for that.

"Heroin is one drug that I will never mess with."

He told me.

I thought that was funny, that this man who was addicted to meth was afraid of heroin. It really was the worst of the worst.
After some time, my friend came into the room, checking on me to make sure I was okay.

How much time had passed?

I wasn't sure.
Once the initial rush calmed down and I felt that I was capable of being in public, I left the hotel and made my way to the party where my friends were waiting, and I spent the rest of the night drinking myself into a blackout as I usually did.
The meth made it easier to keep drinking, and so I did, until the cold harsh reality of the sunrise revealed myself alone, as everyone else was asleep. I resigned that the party was over, and I drove myself home.
As I came down, I knew that I had to get more.
I had a new high to chase, and it quickly became my new obsession.

***

We had been up for days.
My friend and I stood outside the quaint old ranch house in the pitch-black hours of just-before-dawn, smoking a cigarette.
I think he had been up for longer than I had, for he seemed to be losing it quite a bit more than I was.

"Yo, you see those people over there?"

My friend pointed at one of the houses that was down the street from us.

"Dude, what are you talking about?"

I was confused. There was no one there.
My friend was convinced that there was a group of people standing in the front yard at one of the houses, having a BBQ....at 4 AM.
Watching his delusion and hallucination made me feel sick to my stomach. I had watched so many people lose their minds on meth, and I had watched myself lose my own a couple of times as well.
Unable to convince him that there was no one there, I quickly ushered him inside so that he didn't try to go over there and see for himself.
The town we were in was undisturbed and still, not the kind of place that typically has junkies running around in the middle of the night.
I got my friend inside, and we went on with our evening of alternating between shooting up meth to ride that high and shooting up heroin to come down from the meth.

Eventually the dawn broke the horizon, and the guy whose house it was had left for some errands. My friend and I remained behind, sharing the last couple of needles we had left to shoot up with.
When the second to last one clogged and broke, I began to worry that they would all break, and we would be left without a means to ingest our drugs. I'd be damned if I took a drug any other way at that point. I had been shooting up for so long that any attempt to use a drug another way would be a waste-I wouldn't even feel it.
My friend and I argued for some time about the use of the last rig, he was having trouble hitting and I knew this meant there was a risk of it breaking before I could do my shot.

"Just let me hit dude you're gonna clog it."

I pleaded.

"Just one more minute I almost got it."

One more minute became five, and ten, and fifteen.
My heart was racing in fear of not being able to get my shot in.
I kept pleading with him, even reaching for the needle a couple of times. He would dodge my advances, eventually retreating into the bathroom and locking the door so he couldn't be disturbed.

I was banging on the door now, furious. I was desperate. After what felt like forever, he came out. He was just as angry as I was at this point.
We stood face to face in the living room for some time, arguing with each other about the needle. He couldn't see my side and I couldn't see his. Either of us could only see a means to get our next fix and the person who was standing in the way of it.
Push came to shove-literally-and I lunged at him in a blind range. He grabbed me by the arms, deflecting my attack, and pushed me to the ground.
His face twisted up with shock and concern. Me hitting the ground had shaken him enough to stop him from engaging in the fight any longer.
Without another word, he grabbed his coat, and he left out the front door.
I called and texted him, asking where he was going, with no reply.

Looking down at my hand, I realized the needle had broken in the struggle. I let out a defeated, pitiful laugh at how stupid the whole thing was.

Sitting on the couch in silence, the absurd reality of my life weighed heavily on my high. Our friend came home shortly after.

"What happened?"

He asked, referring to the scratch on my face that had happened during the altercation.

I explained the situation, feeling rather stupid and sad about the whole thing.
Hindsight is always clear as day, and some things aren't so pretty in the light.

"Can you take me to my mom's house? I have some extra needles there."

He agreed, and we got in his car. I cracked the window, lighting up a cigarette and noticing the soft luminance of the sun setting all over again.
Where had the day gone?

On this night, I embraced the come down.

***

As I drifted through a darkened state of dreaming, an abrupt bump in the road and muffled *thud* sound suddenly jerked me back to consciousness. I readjusted my hands on the wheel, dazed and unsure of what had just happened. I surveyed my surroundings as I took my foot off the gas, letting the car slowly crawl to a stop. I knew for sure the tire was messed up because it was a battle to hold the wheel straight.

Had I run something over?
Was I asleep?

Switching the car into park, I sat for a minute or two, furiously blinking the sleepiness from my eyes and grasping at my senses. I decided to survey the damage and, stepping out of the car, I walked to the passenger side and inspected the tires.
The front passenger side tire was blown out, and the metal of the wheel was gnarled out of shape and ripped in half.

What did I run over?

Shaking my head at my own foolishness, I got back in my car and glanced at my phone.
It was 5:35 AM.
Too drunk or too ignorant to recognize the implications of what had just happened, I scrolled through my phone and called my mom.

"What?"

My mom's tone of voice accused groggily.

She knew me well enough to know that me calling at this hour meant I had gotten myself into some sort of reckless situation.

"Can you call AAA; I popped a tire."

After a long pause she sighed heavily, still half asleep.

"Yeah sure."

We hung up the phone and I flipped through the radio stations, knowing it would be a while before they got there.
My eyelids weighed heavy as I struggled to stay awake. Despite my best efforts, after a few short minutes, I was passed out cold once more.
About an hour and a half later, I was roused from my drunken sleep just in time for the tow truck to get there. I called my mom once more so she could pick me up.
The driver eyed the tire, then me, wordlessly shaking his head with a look of deep disapproval in his eyes.

Join the club.

I thought to myself, disregarding his disapproval of me.

There was a translucent pink fluid leaked all over the road from under my car, which the driver informed me was the transmission fluid. Not long after the tow truck, my mom pulled up to pick me up. She examined the damage on my car, occasionally throwing daggered looks of disappointment at me upon realizing that "popped a tire" had been a bit of a lie.
Her disappointment and frustration were over my head though, I was half hungover, half drunk, and all I wanted was food and sleep.
Turning back to the driver, my mom instructed him to take the car to a tire shop where we could have the wheel replaced.
I climbed into the safety of the passenger seat of her car to wait and watched as my dad pulled up behind us.

Shit.

I was always in fear of my dad finding out about these things, for while my mom's disapproval of my lifestyle usually came in the form of silent scorn, my dad's reaction was much louder and more abrasive.
He talked with my mom for a bit, looked at the car, glanced quickly at me, and then began to walk along the road the direction that I had come from in an apparent effort to figure out what it was that I had run over.
I watched in the side mirror as his figure shrank into the distance between us.
My mom slipped into the seat next to me with a heavy sigh.

I looked at her face, the shadows cast by the bright light of the sun rising over the plains. She looked so tired, so worn out. I knew that I was responsible for the stress in her life, and my stomach sank with feelings of failure at this realization.

I thought about the time my brother accused me of being responsible for her rapid aging. He said to me that she was getting older, and the stress was killing her.
I was killing her.

She didn't ask me anymore questions, which I was glad. We just sat in silence waiting for my dad to return with the verdict.
The sun was creeping up over the horizon, painting the sky an array of purples, pinks, and oranges.
When my dad returned, he informed us that it looked like I had gone off the road, running over the raised platform that lined the highway, and in doing so had run

over a metal pole which must have scraped underneath my car.

"You must have hit that curb going really fast to cause damage like that."

He eyed me for some sort of reaction.

I nodded, maintaining my silence, and turned to face out the window.
I looked back at my mom,

"Can we go home? I'm starving."

My mom agreed begrudgingly, knowing full well that no amount of lecturing would change anything.

I had come to be regarded as hopeless.

***

The room was cramped with dense, wooden furniture and dimly lit by the antique lamps that sat on either side of the beds. The stodgy, paisley-pattern curtains were pulled tightly shut to keep the darkness in and any unsolicited, wandering eyes out.
The few belongings I had were splayed across the bed, as I had just finished sifting through my bag to find a clean needle.

I barely heard the music and the light conversation going around me as I stuck myself repeatedly, desperately searching for a vein. Blood was seeping from each puncture wound, but I barely noticed. The people I was with would occasionally watch me with pained expressions, offering to help me hit, and I would decline each time, convinced that I could get it myself.
I'm sure it was awful for them to watch me dig at my arms for hours, tweaking out on meth. I desperately needed that shot of heroin to help me come down a little bit.
If I could just get this shot in, I would be fine.

I was with my dealer-who barely spoke English-and one of his "friends," another stray junkie like myself that he had picked up along the way to keep him company as he moved from hotel room to hotel room.
I was sleeping with him, of course. A simple solution to never having any money and always needing drugs. I was always grateful that I was a girl, it was at least a little easier for me to get what I wanted.

I could remember a time when I had these imaginary lines that I told myself I wouldn't cross with my drug use and addiction. Like how I told myself I would never use the needle, or that I wouldn't steal from my family, and that big line, where I told myself I would never trade sex for money or drugs.

Somewhere along the way all those lines that I had drawn in the sand had washed away and long since been crossed, and I found myself teetering at this point of no return. I had forgotten what it was like to hold any sort of boundaries with my addiction, or what it was like to care about what happened to myself at all.

Eventually, out of frustration and impatience, I moved from the bed to the bathroom, feeling insecure about the other two watching me. I'm not sure how long I spent jabbing my arm with that needle, it must have been hours.
Perched on the cold tile floor of the bathroom, when I finally hit, I felt this huge wave of instant relief and relaxation, I felt a little bit closer to a normal human being again.

How long had we been there?

Time was intangible when you never slept.
I struggled to stand up off the bathroom floor, utilizing my hands to brace myself against the sink to steady my frail, shaky legs. Dampening a towel at the bathroom sink, I began to clean the dried blood off my arm and the floor.

Out of the corner of my eye I happened to catch my reflection in the foggy mirror.
Blinking for a few moments, I stared at the stranger who stared back at me under the glaring fluorescent lights.

I did not recognize this girl.

Her hair was stringy and greasy, matted with sweat, pressed against her sharp, jutting cheekbones. Her eyes were sunken in and far away, as if she wasn't there anymore, just a shell.
Graying skin spackled with red marks from picking at the zits that would appear from time to time. If she ever contained a glow, it was long gone now.

Did she remember her family? Did she still love them? Did she even have the capability to love anymore? Any memories of who she used to be were stifled and subdued.

I looked at this girl in the mirror, this stranger, and I felt nothing for her.
I did not feel sorrow, anger, or regret.

I could not feel anything anymore.

***

As the police officer secured the cold metal handcuffs tightly around my thin, bony wrists, the reality of the situation sunk deep into my stomach like a heavy stone sinking deep into the ocean. I felt the weight of the consequences of my actions press down on me and I could not dodge or ignore them any longer.

What have I done?

****

24 hours before my arrest I was the sickest that I'd ever been. I was going through heroin withdrawals from hell alone in my mother's house. She was away on vacation, but my dad would check in on me once or twice a day to make sure I was still alive.

Sometimes I suspected the reason that my dad was so supportive and was always there for me in my addiction was because he felt that he needed to make up for his lack of real fatherhood from when I was a kid.
Either way, I was grateful to have just one person on my side.
And he did not give up on me, even long after I had given up on myself, and though our relationship was always strained, he held me up when I could no longer stand on my own. Most days all I wanted was to just die but knowing how crushed he would have been prevented me from pulling the trigger myself, so instead I waited, day in and day out, and I prayed for God to take me himself.

Lack of sleep distorted my thinking and I found myself slipping into a delusional state as I drank for hours on end to try and numb the pain and skin crawling anxiety that haunted my every waking moment.
On the second night I decided to take a pill of Seroquel- a heavy sedative-in a desperate attempt to knock myself out. I prayed and I prayed for relief, just to be able to sleep at all, even for an hour, but sleep eluded me. Instead, the sleeping pill had me experiencing hallucinations and delirium and at one point I found myself banging on my mom's locked bedroom door, crying for her to take me to the hospital.
I sat crumpled on the carpet floor, sobbing.

"Mom, please."

I cried.

I didn't understand why she wasn't answering the door.

Why wouldn't she help me?

After about 10 minutes of banging on the door and pleading for my mother, I was hit with the sudden realization that she wasn't there… I was hallucinating. She was in another state, on vacation.

There was no one behind that door on which I was banging.

I was alone.

Disoriented, confused, I tried to piece together what was going on, but it seemed the world around me was fragmented and constantly shifting.
I didn't understand what was happening, nor did I understand just how close to death I was at that point. Defeated, I picked myself up off the floor and retreated to my position on the couch and continued to drink myself into a stupor to try and thwart the restlessness of the withdrawals.

I drifted in and out of a semiconscious state until the next morning when my dad stopped by the house to check on me once more. The severity of my situation seemed to hit him when he came over that day and saw that I was too sick to let my dog out and he had gone to bathroom on the floor multiple times. At one point I had stepped in it and was too out of it to clean my foot off.

Concern was etched deep in the wrinkles on his face, and he began calling friends and family to see if they had any left-over pain pills,

"Just to take the edge off."

He explained.

I certainly never thought that I would see the day when my dad would try and help me score drugs. Things must have been bad for him to get to this point.

We were having no luck with this and at one point he even carted me off to the methadone clinic to see if there was anything they could do.

They explained in an annoyingly calm and collected way that I would have to make an appointment to get evaluated by the doctor first; there was nothing they could do to help me in that moment.
We drove back home in silence and my hope for relief was dwindling. I had to figure out a way to get high; the wheels in my fogged-up brain began to turn.
A plan had been formed by the time we got back home- it even seemed like a good one at the time.

I called one of my dealers up and asked him to meet somewhere, knowing full well I had no money and that my intention was to rob him.
I told my dad we were going to meet someone who would give me Suboxone-a drug like methadone that would stop the withdrawals.
Pausing for a moment and eyeing me suspiciously, he told me if I got out of his truck when we got there that he would leave me there and he would be done trying to help me.

The thing is, when you are that sick and in that state of mind that is pure survival mode, nothing else matters aside from getting well.
You don't think about consequences, you don't think about what will happen afterwards, only relief.

I once heard someone describe heroin withdrawals like this:

“It’s like when you’re a kid at the pool and you have one of those breath holding competitions with your friends. You sink down into the water and you hold your breath for as long as you can take, then there’s this feeling, a moment where your whole body is screaming for oxygen, every fiber of your being.
Survival mode kicks in as you just can’t take it anymore and you swim up to take a breath.

That feeling-that moment of not being able to take it anymore-of your whole body screaming for air, you feel like you’re dying-that’s how it feels.”

We arrived at the location where my dealer agreed to meet and not one second after putting his truck in park, I made a move for the door handle.

“Sarah if you get out of this truck, I’m done.”

My dad warned.

I looked at him; I knew he meant it. I knew that what I was doing was the wrong decision, but I could do nothing to stop myself. I did not feel like I had a choice anymore. The scenario in which I remained in the car and returned home flashed through my mind, but my consideration was fleeting. I could not go back to that house, I had to get relief. I opened the door and got out of the truck. I watched my dad’s heart break as he watched me make my decision, and, keeping his promise, I listened as he drove away, but I did not turn to watch him go.

I walked over to the entrance of the store and sat on the benches, calling the dealer repeatedly. Fear gripped my heart as each call went unanswered. My mind was racing; was he blowing me off?

I desperately tried to come up with a solution-what was I going to do?

People walked by, glancing at me with pity as they did. I was a mess.
It was the very end of May, and I was wearing shorts, knee-high black boots that zipped up on the side, and my oldest brother's shaggy winter coat that fit me like a dress, ending just above my knees. My hair-at one point tied up in a ponytail-was now a tangled rat's nest atop my head. My clothes hung off my bones and stuck to my clammy, grey skin.
I looked homeless, and I guess, in that moment I was.

After about an hour of waiting and waiting I knew in the pit of my stomach that he wasn't going to come. He probably sensed that I was lying about having any money.
The audacity, for him to not show up so that I could rob him.

I sat there outside this grocery store in full blown heroin withdrawals with nothing but the clothes on my back, a dead phone, and half a pack of cigarettes. I felt very much like a wild animal that had been backed into a

corner. Scared, alone, and desperate, my ideas of how to get out of this situation were far from reasonable.
For quite some time I remained the bench outside, sweating in my winter coat in the 80-degree heat, watching the people walk in and out of the store. If I had been capable of feeling anything at all, I probably would have cried. But in that moment, I was reduced to something less than human, nothing but pure survival instinct.

The hopelessness that I felt in that moment trumped any sort of period of consideration for consequences one might go through when they are about to commit a crime. There was no second thought, I did not feel as though I had a choice.

Coming to terms with my fate, I walked through the store, scanning the people around me when I spotted a woman standing in line to check out. Her purse was in the grocery cart behind her, and she stood facing the other way. I didn't have a plan, I barely knew what it was that I was going to do, I simply reacted to this moment of opportunity.
I grabbed the purse, and I shoved it in my jacket as I walked quickly out of the store. My heart was racing, fueled by pure adrenaline.

I knew I had to get out of there fast, so I matched the key in the purse to an old Ford pickup in the parking lot and I slid the key into the lock.
I had the door cracked slightly open when I looked towards the front of the store and saw the woman

running outside frantically. She looked towards her car and in that moment, we locked eyes with each other.

That was it, I knew that I was finished.

I did not try to run as she walked over to me, and I handed her the purse back.
I don't remember exactly what she said to me in that moment, but I told her I was sorry, and she told me she was sorry for me, for whatever it was that I was going through.

It struck me-the compassion that this woman had for me despite me trying to steal from her. I felt like she saw me for me, just a scared, lost little girl. She chose to see past the pathetic junkie that most people would chalk me up to be when they looked at me.

The world around me was spinning too fast, I could not think, and I felt I was going to pass out as I walked away from her truck. Several bystanders followed me as I continued to walk along the strip mall, I could hear them talking to the police on the phone.
I had already given up any sort of fight for my freedom at this point. I was exhausted.
I found some chairs and a table, and I sat down, lighting a cigarette. I felt this wave of complete acceptance wash over me. A moment of surrender, I gave in to my fate. Only a few minutes had passed before the cops arrived in several cars and they surrounded me where I sat at the table.

"Ma'am, what are you doing?"

One of the officers asked me.

"Smoking a cigarette."

I replied.

They told me to put the cigarette out and stand up and I obliged.

I considered for a moment that if I were in jail then at least I would be able to get medical treatment for the withdrawals and that seemed alright to me. Much better than wandering the streets and sleeping in a park.
A few of the officers rifled through my few belongings and barked questions at me while the others spoke with the witnesses who confirmed that I was the one who had committed the crime. I'm not sure if the severity of the situation had really sunk in yet, right up until the sobering moment that they placed the cold metal handcuffs around my wrists and told me that I was under arrest.

Part of me still felt like that teenager who on numerous occasions was simply written a ticket and released to my parents. I was not capable of comprehending what was happening.
I wanted to go home, but that was not an option this time. I wasn't a kid anymore.

I spent the next 4 days slowly deteriorating on the floor of the jail cell in medical. I was too sick to care about whether I got bonded out, I was too sick to care about

much of anything at all. I had accepted my fate and I no longer cared whether I lived or died.
My cellmates seemed to have more regard for my wellbeing than I did because they began pressing the call button in the cell to summon the nurses.

"Yo, you guys need to help this girl or she's gonna die."

One of my cellmates called for the nurse through the intercom.

She was a heroin addict too-and she was 6 months pregnant with twins. Because of this, the officers would cart her off to the methadone clinic every morning so that the opiate withdrawals didn't harm the babies.
She was pretty and seemed like a nice enough person. I wondered how she got to where she was, sitting in that jail cell with me. I guess people probably thought the same thing about me, too.
I felt this weird sense of gratitude for these strangers I shared a cell with. I was grateful that someone cared about me and wanted to help me.

Despite numerous different medications I continued to throw up about every 15 minutes or so, until I eventually became so dehydrated that my muscles began contracting and seizing up.
On one of my frequent escorted visits to the nurse's station I showed the nurse on duty my hands which were clenched together like the claws of a crab, and I told her I couldn't move them, asking her what that meant.
She looked down at my hands and examined them,

"How long have they been like that?"

She asked.

"Since yesterday, I think."

She nodded slowly, considering for a moment the situation, then, explaining that she would be right back, she left the room briefly to speak with the doctor. When she returned, she explained to me that they were calling an ambulance and I would be taken to the hospital.
I barely comprehended the words that she was saying to me as she explained that the severity of my dehydration was life threatening.

I sat in the nurse's station for several minutes until the ambulance arrived. The EMT's came in and spoke with the nurse briefly, getting as much information about my condition as possible. I couldn't help but notice how they spoke to the nurse, and not to me. It was as if I wasn't even in the room.
As they wheeled me out on the stretcher, I felt a sense of comfort knowing that they would take better care of me at the hospital. I counted the lights on the ceiling as I passed underneath them.
Opening and closing my eyes, I drifted in and out of awareness.

Apparently being taken to the hospital in an ambulance from jail is exciting stuff for everyone, for they all gawked at me, wondering what was going on. I pretended not to notice.

I spent a day in the ER, chained to the bed with two officers in my room making casual conversation while the nurses pumped me full of IV fluids and other medications to ease the pain of the withdrawals.

I drifted in and out of sleep, occasionally roused by the sound of the officers speaking softly in the room with me, or by a nurse coming to check my vitals.
I enjoyed being at the hospital, being taken care of. Despite being shackled up like a criminal the nurses there were genuinely nice to me. They seemed genuinely concerned for my well-being, unlike many of the doctors I had encountered in the past who looked at me with disgust.
They were always too convinced that I was only there to score drugs to hear what I had to say.

My stay in the ER was all too brief and when they decided I was improved enough, I returned to my jail cell, where they administered a dose of Suboxone. Taking the strips from the doctor through the door, I placed the medicine under my tongue and shuffled back to my bed.
I laid there on the floor of my cell, feeling the creeping sensation of the dissipating withdrawals wash over me. What felt like only a few moments later,

"Blair."

One of the guards called for me.

"You've been bonded out."

I was hit with a bittersweet mixture of relief and indifference.
It's not like my life outside of that jail cell was anything to look forward to. It had been a long time since I had looked forward to anything other than the next high.
A part of me felt like I had nothing to get out to; no place felt like home anymore.

I made it through the long and arduous process of being released to find my father waiting for me. I was not surprised to see him-he was always there to bail me out of whatever mess I had gotten myself into. Despite our differences and years of a strained relationship one thing I knew for certain: my dad loved me, and he only wanted the best for me.

I hopped up into his truck and we made our way back home. I watched out the window as the world went by. The sun was setting below the mountains, and everything was bathed in that dreamy light they refer to as "The Golden Hour."

My dad and I drove home in silence.
I was grateful for that.

***

12

I still remember what I was wearing the night I met him. A black tank top, tucked into a knee length pencil skirt that was striped white and navy blue. My hair was pulled back in a neat ponytail, and on my feet were white lace flats.

Through a series of unexpected events, I found myself boarding a plane to Las Vegas with the intention of meeting a friend there. She was my closest friend at the time-the only one who seemed tolerate my addiction. With her, I functioned as a black hole, swallowing her into my darkness and pulling her down with me. The longer we hung out the more often she would ask me to share whatever I had, and I always did.
She was there on a work trip; she worked the front desk at a small eye doctors office in town and that weekend Las Vegas was hosting some convention for eye doctors. For whatever reason, she decided to invite me.

I was grateful to be getting away from everything for a few days, completely ignoring the fact that I was out on bond and not allowed to leave the state. Failing to consider the consequences as I so often did, I took the risk, and I boarded the plane.

Within an hour of arriving in Las Vegas, I proceeded to get blacked out drunk. The last thing I remember is taking swigs out of a bottle of rum at the airport while I waited for my friend to land, since we had taken different flights.

Late the next morning, I reluctantly peeled my eyes open, squinting them tightly against the harsh light of day. My head was pounding, my mouth was bone dry, and my body felt like I had slept for a hundred years. Sitting up in bed, my friend and I laughed together at my stupidity when she told me the story of me running around the hotel barefoot, rolling up balls of tin foil and throwing them at the other guests.

My friend went to her convention for the day, and I quickly got to work in finding what I needed. I smoked the little heroin I had brought with me off foil, knowing that I would have to get syringes, for smoking it was not enough. It took me only about 3 hours to find both heroin, and cocaine-I was always quite resourceful when it came to these things.

Pacing down the strip, the still-blazing, late September sun stung my scalp. I made my way to the local pharmacy to pick up some needles and I strolled back to the hotel.

Retreating to the air-conditioned room, I fell into my routine of making up a shot with my supplies and injecting the drugs.

Heroin was the best cure for a hangover.

When the first day of the convention was over, myself, my friend, and her coworkers all met up with another group that was there for the same work convention, and we all went out to eat at an upscale French restaurant located inside of another one of the resorts that decorated the strip.
Walking inside the building, my attention was immediately pulled in by the ceiling. It looked as though the ceiling inside the resort lobby was a 3-dimensional sky, with twinkling stars peeking out behind softly swaying clouds.
It was beautiful.

I started off dinner taking shots with the rest of the group, all the while glancing across the table at one of the guys who was along with the other group.
Looking at him was like coming home, like being safe for the first time. He was perfect, and I knew from the moment that I saw him that not only did I need him, but I would have him.

About halfway through dinner, I excused myself outside to smoke a cigarette, the night air was warm and dry. I lit my cigarette. Inhaling deeply, I glanced around, taking in all the lights, feeling the warmth of the alcohol stirring in my stomach and dizzying my mind. I silently cursed myself for taking so many shots so fast and I was grateful for the moment of peace and quiet away from the table and the crowd so that I could collect myself.

I often felt like I was drifting through life and every now and then I would stop and look around and ask myself how it was that I got there-to that moment.
I never had an answer.
I never knew where I was going, either.

My friend followed behind me shortly after and leaned in front of me as I lit her cigarette as well. We stood side by side and I told her about my newfound crush and my intentions to sleep with him.

She laughed when I told her I always get what I want.
She must have thought I was joking.
We finished our cigarette and our conversation and returned to the table.

Sometime around the end of the dinner, the rest of the night escaped me as I slipped into another black out, though bits and pieces of the night remained fragmented in my memory.

Blackness.
Getting back to the hotel.
Blackness.
Shooting up cocaine in the hotel room.
Blackness.
Him.

When did he get there?

His body on mine, his heart and mine.

Blackness.

I awoke the next morning very slowly, struggling to pull myself out of the fog and piece together the night before. I sensed a body lying next to me and I looked over to see him there, sleeping.
He felt so familiar, had he always been there?

I glanced at the clock and my heart dropped.

"Shit."

I muttered as I ripped the covers off the bed and began rushing around the room, throwing all my belongings into my suitcase in a frenzy.

My flight was to leave in 2 hours, and I was not the slightest bit ready.
The commotion I was making stirred both him and my friend from their sleep, and they helped me get all my things together to fly back home.
I rushed downstairs into the lobby and out the front door to hail a cab.
He and my friend trailed behind me, chatting our small talk, and saying our goodbyes.

I put my things in the cab and turned to face him.
I could not wrap my head around the possibility that I would never see him again, and he must have felt the same because he gave me his number.

"I had fun last night."

I looked into his eyes, and I prayed that he meant it when he said we would see each other again.
I kissed him and fell into the cab.
We pulled away from the hotel and I watched out the window as his figure disappeared behind me.

***

"One is too many and a thousand is never enough."

How long had I been sitting on this couch?
When did these girls get here?

They were both equally, exceptionally beautiful.
They were elegant, with long legs adorned with fishnet stockings and stiletto heels, hair done up and makeup perfect.
One of them was wearing a fluffy pink fur coat that inspired thoughts of royalty.
They laughed and talked with each other and our mutual friend, whose house we had been partying in for days.
At one point-before the drugs had taken what was inevitably owed to them-he had been a very handsome man. He was a videographer by hobby, and his latest obsession was to make short films and videos depicting our lifestyle.

The house was a mess, dishes piled in the sink, the fridge was full of beer with truly little food, and none of us ever bothered to clean anything. Dust and dirt accumulated in every corner and all the furniture in the house was old, beat up, and grungy. Most of which we had found in alleyways-someone else's trash.
The house may have been a disaster, but it was a sure spot to hang out and get high for as long as you wanted to.

I was a trap house.

I pulled my attention back from my thoughts and observations, returning to the room and reaching into my bag to fish out the tools to load another shot. I was feeling a little too relaxed from the heroin and needed a boost of the meth to keep from falling out.
I tapped the small plastic bag and watched as several shards of glass fell into the tin. With the dropper I measured out a small amount of water and, using the plunger of the needle, crushed up the meth and mixed it in with the water.
The liquid mixture had a phosphorescent tint to it, gleaming under the red light of the lamp beside me.
I dropped a small piece of cotton into the tin and sucked up the clear liquid with the syringe.
I had done this routine so many times it was like second nature, muscle memory.
I could load a shot with my eyes closed.

I never needed a tourniquet-somehow my veins stayed "good"- so I just sunk the needle into my skin and pushed the liquid fire into my veins. I felt the deep burn and ache as the poison moved up my arm inside the bloodstream, my heart stuttered, and I coughed as the ether rose in my chest.

It hit me like a wave.

I took a deep breath, bracing for the ride, feeling my hands and feet start to sweat and I looked around as the other two girls in the room did their shots as well. Our friend stood by with the camera, waiting to record the moment when the drugs hit.
Heart pounding, I lit my cigarette and took a long, deep drag and watched as he got a close-up of one of their faces right after she had done her shot. A slow and steady smile crept across when the drug came over her. There was music playing somewhere, the kind you hear in a dark, underground club, down a flight of stone steps behind an unmarked door.

It was intense. It was strange and dark and yet it was just another day for me.
I continued to sit on that ratty old couch for days as people came and went, they would stay for a day and party with us and then they would be gone.

And I would remain, watching the world go by around me.

***

I was dope sick, as usual.

I sometimes joked that I was not particularly good at being a drug addict, for I could never seem to make the bags last long enough to skirt the withdrawals.
Though it never worked, and made things worse, I had been shooting up cocaine for hours at a friend's house while we waited for the guy to be ready to go get what I needed.
He did not use heroin, so he didn't know what I was feeling.

Lucky him.

I lay on the bed, sickly and sweating, heart racing from the cocaine as someone in the room flipped through the music.
A song came on and I found myself enthralled by the sound.
I lost myself in the lyrics and it stirred long-lost emotions in me as I listened to the man in the speaker sing,

"…slowly drifting,
drifting away,
and it feels like I'm drowning…"

I could not help but feel that the song gave a voice to what my addiction felt like.
Being pulled out to sea, drifting away, feeling like I was drowning.

The hour finally came when the dealer was ready, and we began our long, arduous journey across town on the bus. It was freezing outside, the bitter, dry, March air stealing your breath from your lungs.
People on the bus kept glancing at me nervously. I was not sure if I looked as bad as I felt or if the coke was just making me paranoid, but I tried to take deep breaths to steady my shaky nerves.

We transferred from one bus to another in what felt like hours and hours, and we ran into a friend there.
I drifted in and out of presence as I listened to their conversation. The new guy looked at me.

"You sick or what?"

"Yeah, super fucking sick."

He asked me how long I had been withdrawing and I told him almost 24 hours.

"Damn, that's brutal."

A heroin addict himself, he empathized with me.
So much so that he offered to give me a shot.
I felt like I had won the lottery, running into this man on the bus and him being unusually generous for an addict- we usually did not like to share.

"Come on."

He beckoned as we hopped off the bus a few stops short of our destination, and we walked over to the library.
He went into the men's room for several minutes as I waited outside the door, sweating under the fluorescent lighting and avoiding eye contact with those who passed by.
Coming back out, he handed me a loaded rig with his hand facing down, sneakily slipping it into mine where no one would see.

I barely contained my excitement as I went into the bathroom to get well.
To my dismay and frustration, I couldn't get a vein.
I was too sick, too dehydrated to find a vein.

I must have been in the bathroom for an extended period because he poked his head in to make sure I was alright- that I hadn't fallen out.

"Yeah, I can't get a hit."

I told him.

We both feared drawing attention to ourselves, so we left the library and walked a little way in the cold to a secluded area under a bridge.
There was trash littered about the ground, graffiti painted on the walls, and no one else around.

"Just do a muscle shot, I do it all the time."

He tried to help me as I frustratingly continued to find a vein.
I was afraid to do the muscle shot, for fear of an abscess, but after what may have been an hour of failed attempts, I agreed.
I sat next to the creek and gazed into the rushing water as he stuck the needle into my shoulder muscle.
To my surprise, there was no burn like there usually was when you missed. Far enough into the muscle, I couldn't even feel it.
I did feel the withdrawals begin to melt away, though, and I could have cried with relief.

We parted ways, my friend and I continued our journey, eventually finding ourselves at our destination.

He bought me what I needed and as I sat in the bathroom loading up another shot, I wondered to myself how long it had been since I had been home.

***

A couple of months after Vegas, the boy and I had begun to hang out on a regular basis. I guess you could say that we were together at that point. He was perfect, and I was madly in love with him.

Looking at him, I would sit in awe and wonder how it was that this man chose me, that he wanted anything to do with me.

Granted, he didn't really know about my addiction, because of course I lied. I told him that I used to use, but that I was sober now. I did everything that I could to maintain this mask that I wore for him, I wanted so badly for the person I pretended to be to be real. I thought that maybe if I tried hard enough to convince myself, and him, that I could be the woman that he needed, that maybe it would happen, maybe I *would* become her.

Mostly I just found myself exhausted from the web of lies that I had to maintain. Why I couldn't hold a job, why I was losing weight, why I would disappear for hours on end, repeatedly saying that I would be there soon.
It broke my heart to lie to him, and it broke my heart even more that he believed it. He had so much faith in me, and I never deserved it.

Sitting on the couch one day, I studied his face as he watched the hockey game. He was such a beautiful man. Dark brown-almost black hair, deep green eyes, and a strong, sharp jawline. I studied his body, he was so strong and solid, and made me feel so small.
I felt safe with him, in a way that I had never felt before. He had seen all the worst parts of me-well, almost-and he still loved me and wanted me around.
I didn't understand how when I could hardly stand to be around myself.

Threading my arm underneath his and wrapping my fingers around his bicep, admiring the tattoos that covered his body, I traced the outline of them with my finger. Resting my head on his shoulder I sighed deeply, my heart heavy with shame.
He turned his head and looked at me, kissing the top of my head.

I think he liked the way that I needed him, and I did need him-badly.
I wanted so desperately to be better for him, he deserved so much better than who I was capable of being.
I just couldn't figure out how to stop.
I felt as though I were caught between the two great loves of my life- him, and heroin.

I stood in between these two worlds, torn in two pieces as I could not bring myself let go of either one.

***

13

There were so many moments I swore to myself, and to the people in my life, that I'd never do it again, and even though each time I meant it when I said it, I always found myself back in the grips of my addiction, wondering how I'd managed to get there.

I arrived home from one of my daily excursions to get what I needed, and I flopped down on my bed. I had enough dope to keep me well for the next 24 hours and so, for the moment, I was content.
Eyes closed, I began to drift into a state of careless bliss when my phone rang, pulling me out of my stupor.

It was my dad; he called me almost every day to check on me. Even when my mom would kick me out and I would be staying on couches in trap houses.

On that afternoon, I picked up the phone rather than ignoring it like I would have if I were out doing things that I shouldn't. The way I saw it, if I was home, I didn't have to deal with the guilt of him worrying if I was okay.

We talked for a while, and then there was a pause.

"Sarah,"

Another pause. I could feel him searching for the words on the other end of the phone.

"I have cancer."

His voice cracked as he choked up with tears.
I had never seen or heard my dad cry before.

I felt my stomach in my throat as my brain struggled to find its way out of the fog to try and grasp the words that my father had just spoke.

"Well.... are you okay? What does that mean? What kind of cancer?"

I stumbled over the questions; I did not know what to say, what to think, or how to feel.
His answers to my questions were vague and our conversation after that was brief.
My dad was never good at talking about how he felt or about anything that was difficult.
I guess I inherited that trait from him.

I hung up the phone and set it down on the bed next to me. I continued to lay there, and I just stared at the ceiling for a while.... waiting.
I guess I was waiting for the wave of emotions you expect to hit you in the moment that your dad tells you that he's going to die. Waiting for the tears to burn my eyes and roll down my cheeks in a never-ending stream. Waiting for any sort of reaction at all.
The emotions did not come, nor did the tears, though I could feel them festering just below the surface.

I knew that nothing would ever be the same. My world as I had always known it had ended.
I practiced telling people that my dad had cancer in my head. It didn't seem real, the words felt alien to me as though they belonged to someone else.

I'd never felt the selfishness of my addiction as acutely as I did in the days following my dad's revelation. After my dad telling us he had cancer, my mom and brothers kept asking ME if I was okay. They were all worried about me when they should have been focusing on him. I guess my lack of reaction to the situation had them concerned for my well-being and what I might do next. They tip-toed around me as though I were a landmine just waiting to explode.

I guess I understood where they were coming from. I was already prone to self-destruction, and they feared that this diagnosis would send me off the deep end from which I would never return.

I felt gross.

My father was dying and yet everyone was worried about me and whether I would be okay.

I saw myself and my actions for what they were and for the first time in my life I really wished that things were different.

I wanted to be better than that.

I just didn't know how.

***

The soft light of the afternoon sun was settling through the blinds of my window, warming my room with a hazy glow. Tiny specks of dust set ablaze in the light, floating aimlessly through the air.

The house was quiet, the only thing I could hear was the occasional muffled sounds of my mom shuffling around downstairs.
I sat on my bed, carefully breaking off pieces of heroin from my bag and placing them in the metal cooker. I could smell the pungent vinegar scent of the drugs, and it made my heart skip with anticipation.
The smell became so familiar, always triggering feelings of comfort within me.
That day was one of the easier ones; I had enough to last me until the next day.

Oftentimes I would awaken in an immediate panic, mind racing with thoughts of how much I had left and what I would have to do that day to get more.
My entire existence revolved around getting money, getting the drugs, and doing whatever I had to do to not be dope sick.

I loaded up the shot, and carefully peeled back my shirt sleeve to reveal an arm full of track marks, bruising, and dried blood that I didn't care enough to clean off.
With the syringe placed between my teeth, I used the pointer finger of my other hand to feel for a vein that would be suitable.
Going in my usual spot on the inside of my arm just above the wrist, I sunk the needle into the skin, pulling it back and pushing it in to adjust the depth until I saw the little red spurt of blood come through-alerting me that I had struck gold.
Operating out of autopilot and muscle memory, I pushed the drug in and pulled the needle out, licking off the droplets of blood that seeped out.

Leaning back, I sighed deeply as I began to taste a hint of the drug on my tongue.
The rush was intense, and I felt my skin prickle, my scalp began to itch, and I felt dizzy.
Immediately, some sort of deeper instinct kicked in, and something inside of me told me that I had done too much.
I sprang into action, feeling the heavy blanket of an overdose settling down on me.
I stood up off my bed on shaky, weak legs. Placing my hand against the wall, I held myself up, forcing myself to stay standing.

"Shit."

My mind was foggy, and every action I took seemed to be my survival instincts taking control.
I had watched at least five people overdose in front of me at this point, so I was no stranger to it.
Pulling out another one of my usual foxhole prayers, I asked God to help me, promising nothing in return.

Standing there for what felt like hours, I used all my strength to remain upright, desperately keeping my eyes open. I knew that if I were laying or sitting down, I would fall out.

After some time, the haze began to lift, and my head felt increasingly clear. I felt that I was relatively safe at that point, so I returned to my position on the bed.

The sun was mostly set, and the room was getting dark.

I could hear my mom making dinner downstairs.

***

Sick again, I was somewhere around the 12th hour of withdrawals. I spent most of the night crawling around on my hands and knees, scouring the carpet, desperate to find even a crumb of heroin to ease the pain I was in. Scheming up a plan as usual, I arranged to meet a friend to trade some of the meth I had for heroin so that I could get well.

In the weeks before this night my mother and I had numerous discussions about one last attempt at getting me sober, it was now, or never-she made that abundantly clear to me. I knew that she meant it this time, and somewhere inside of me I knew that it was true for me too. I was either going to get sober this time or give in to a short and miserable life of drug addiction.
I set out on my journey to feel better- I had to walk about a mile away to meet with this friend and do the trade.

I was sickly looking-I hadn't showered in at least a week, there were various splotches of blood stained on my torn-up jeans from shooting up. My clothes hung off my boney limbs loosely, slipping off my shoulders and hips, needing constant readjustments.
Junkies don't really consider things like belts.
It must have been over a month since I last brushed my teeth. I no longer had the capacity to care about how I looked. The only thing I could manage to apply my energy to was to find money for drugs. I was a sad, sorry excuse for a human being.

My blood pressure was so high from the withdrawals I thought the walk alone would kill me. I had to stop periodically to try and catch my breath and calm my racing heart, often wondering if I would even make it there.

A part of me hoped that this was it, the moment that the drugs would finally kill me.
I think somewhere deep down, a part of me was always hoping for that.

I continued down the sidewalk, knowing that relief was only several minutes away. I tried to keep my gaze on the pavement directly in front of me, afraid that if I broke focus on my feet that I would stumble and fall. I hadn't slept in days, and between that, the lack of food, and the withdrawals, I was barely functioning.
I looked up from my fixation on the pavement in front of me and saw a young couple about a hundred yards ahead of me-they were walking towards me on the same sidewalk. I felt so ashamed about my appearance, even hiding behind dark sunglasses. I wished that I were invisible.

I cannot imagine what I looked like to this couple-it couldn't have been anything good-and I couldn't help but notice when they crossed the street to avoid walking next to me.
I wanted to cry. I wanted to yell at these people and tell them that I wasn't a bad person, that they didn't need to be afraid of me. My heart was heavy, their judgements weighed on me, making my skin itch.

I did not want to be this way anymore; I cursed my own existence and my inability to change it.
Still, I continued to walk; my weary feet carrying me against my will. There was no fight left in me.

When I finally made it to my destination and back, I collapsed on to the couch, gathering up all my supplies to load the shot. I sat there for a while just struggling to breathe, feeling the sweat roll down my face. I thought my heart would explode, or maybe it had already.
Like a placebo, I felt better already just knowing that I had what I needed in hand.

I pressed the needle into the inner side of my wrist and adjusted the depth until I saw it register blood. With a deep sigh I slowly pushed the amber colored fluid into my veins. I sat there, needle in hand, staring out the window. As I felt the withdrawals slowly melting away, something else happened-or rather-didn't happen.
For the first time, I did not feel any sort of relief from the drug.
The emptiness in me remained a gaping hole.

Some part of me in that moment wondered if this is all my life would ever amount to. I wished for death, yet I knew on a deeper level that death would not come for me, I would only keep on the way that I was for many years to come.
It wasn't death that scared me-it was the thought of having to keep living the way that I was living that scared me.
For the first time I was able to see myself in a brutally honest light. I was turning into a sociopath-that I was sure of. I no longer felt anything other than basic survival instincts-and the only thing that I felt I needed to survive anymore was the drugs. Before food, before water or hygiene or a roof over my head, before anything else, I needed the drugs.

I felt as though a bright white light shone on every dark corner of my life and I was able to see things for what they were-for what they would become.
The life that was revealed to me was cold, empty, ugly.

I knew somewhere inside of me that this was it-I was done.

***

Lost somewhere in between the oppression of night and the soft break of daylight, I sat. So many nights I sat awake like this as the world around me slept and wandered about within their dreams.
I would be going to detox in the morning. I did not feel hopeful, nor did I feel afraid.
I was just existing.
Nothing more.

My phone rang suddenly, and I glanced down at the illuminated screen to see who the caller was. I was shocked to see the name on the phone, it was my friend- the one who had overdosed and almost died next to me. I hadn't spoken with her in years after what had happened that night, and I didn't blame her for the silence between us.
I wouldn't want to associate with someone like me, either.
I answered the phone, my heart filled with fear as I prepared for a lecture or some speech telling me what a horrible person I was.

Those kinds of conversations were common for me at that time in my life.
At some point along the way I had a "friend" tell me they hoped that I would overdose and die. I looked down at my phone as I read that message, blinking at the words in the text, thinking to myself,

"Me too."

As I listened to her speak, it was clear by the slurred speech and broken sentences that my friend was drunk.

We spent a rather brief period engaging in meaningless small talk, the usual: "How are you," "Good how are you," sort of thing, and then there was a moment of silence,

"Sarah, I need you to know that what happened that night wasn't your fault."

Her words rang in my ears, dancing around in my head as I struggled to fathom this foreign concept of forgiveness. It was not something that had been offered to me for a long time, if ever.

Amid my stunned silence, she went on to explain that she was sorry for how everything had happened; she was sorry for the way that our friendship had ended, and that she never blamed me for the overdose.
I listened, taking every word in as I struggled to come up with what I could say that would adequately express my gratitude.

After a short while we said our goodbyes and she wished me luck. I lowered the phone from my ear, dumbfounded.
I could not think of a better time to have heard those words than the time that she had chosen to say them to me.
Tears welled up just behind the whites of my eyes, a sharp and familiar sting.
It had been a long time since I had cried, I couldn't even remember the last time.

I watched the sun rise that morning feeling as though there might finally be an end to the darkness, and it had never felt more like a new day than it did in that moment.

A quiet peace came over me.

***

I clung to him as though I were clinging on to the last thing in my life that made me feel normal, made me feel okay.
I loved him, and for reasons I didn't understand, he loved me.
We loved each other the way two dying people who are desperate for more time stay holding on. We were sick together, him with his drinking, and me with my drugs. Although, he always maintained some semblance of denial regarding my addiction, even though I had lost roughly forty pounds over the course of our 9 months together.

Still, despite all the crazy and the codependence, he was the only thing onto which I was holding. If it weren't for him, I would have let myself be washed away by the tides of my disease long ago. He gave me a tiny glimmer of hope, the smallest bit of desire to be better. I was grateful for that.

Eventually, as time flushed out the darkest of our secrets and the cold ugly truth of my addiction became known, I found myself detoxing at his apartment. No longer able to maintain that I "didn't have a problem."

He had taken a few days off work to help see me through the worst of it, I felt that he was in over his head. I drank to ease the withdrawals and he drank to ease his own demons and he would pass out for some time as I paced the apartment, desperate to jump out of my skin.

I looked at him as he slept, I loved him so much. He cared for me so much and only wanted to help me get better, I could see that.
But I was so sick and so weak, I didn't want to feel this way anymore. Any resolve to get sober had died long ago, I felt hopeless.

I retreated to the parking garage to choke down another cigarette, hoping that the fresh air would help ease the restlessness. I was crouched down on the ground, sweating, sniffling, and praying for God to take my life. Having woken from his sleep, he came out and took a seat on the ground next to me, lighting his own cigarette. I looked at him, tears in my eyes.

"I can't do this, I'm so sick."

I began to cry.

"Yes, you can."

I hated the way he was so sure, especially when he had no idea how this felt. He began to offer suggestions to help, like detox.

"I can't even walk, I'm too weak, how am I supposed to get to a detox?"

Shaking my head, I wiped the sweat and the tears from my face.

"I'll carry you."

He replied.

I continued to cry. His love made me want to hold on, but I had no strength left.

I couldn't be the woman he wanted, the woman he needed.
It was useless.

We went back into the apartment, and I drank some more, and sometime later that day he fell asleep again, I passed out briefly next to him and when I awoke, still sick, I dug through his pockets and I stole his iPod, took it to a pawn shop, and got high.

Returning to his apartment, I laid down next to him as he slept, and I looked at this man that I knew I didn't deserve.
I felt relief to not be sick anymore, but guilt and shame flooded every corner of my heart.
I had never stolen from him before, until now.
He never asked about the fact that I suddenly wasn't sick anymore.

Denial can be a comfortable place to exist.

***

In the beginning, the darkness and nothingness of the drugs brought comfortable silence from the raging storms inside my head and my heart. I found solace in the emptiness.

I wanted so badly for the pain to stop that feeling nothing at all seemed a suitable alternative-and I would stop at nothing to maintain this delusion.

I once turned to drugs and alcohol because I felt as though I had no control over my emotions, that they dominated my existence, and I was a slave to whatever mood happened to strike me in any given moment.

I became convinced that drugs and alcohol gave me that control back, but the truth that I failed to see was that I had only handed over the reins of "control" to my addiction and that I remained powerless.

I so desperately wanted the ache in my heart to cease. Eventually my addiction took everything away; it was a soul crushing void that swallowed up everything that I loved. Little by little, all the pieces of me that once made me whole began to chip away until there was next to nothing left.

I had reached this point where not even the drugs could soothe the emptiness inside of me. I felt as though I had been traveling on this road for far too long and I had finally reached the end.

I stared into the void that lay before me.

I gazed out at the darkness; I knew I could not turn back. The only option left was for me to jump.

***

That night I was up-like so many nights before-restless in my bones, praying for an escape from the misery that I felt, sweating out the last few days of the withdrawals. I paced from the couch to the garage, smoking countless cigarettes in a desperate attempt to distract from the horrible terror and anxiety that crawled around beneath my skin.

I tried to distract my mind with whatever infomercial and garbage television happened to be on at that hour. It was like this recurring nightmare that I found myself stuck in so many times before.

"How did I get here, again?"

I begged the question to which I did not have the answer.

I thought about my family, I wondered if they genuinely believed in my ability to kick it this time or if they were just clinging to some sense of false hope. Perhaps they were just as delusional as I was, thinking that I could ever change.

As for me, any small sliver of hope that things would ever be different had withered and faded away long ago.

Despite the death of any lingering sense of self-worth, I had tried to go to detox at my mother's plea, but after two short days I was discharged-my insurance had stopped paying.
My mom came and picked me up, she seemed so defeated that car ride home, and I felt the same.

My mom desperately called various treatment centers trying to find a place for me to go. I was slumped in the seat next to her, staring out the window only half tuned in to her talking.
I had officially given up, surrendered to my fate, and waited for the waves to wash me away entirely. I longed to be pulled out to sea, into the depths and the darkness of the water.
We made it back to her house just in time for the medication they had given me at detox to begin wearing off. I began to drink in a vain attempt to ease the pain. It never worked, and I never stopped trying.

The house lay still. I walked upstairs to my room; each step forward as heavy as a hammer to a nail, sealing my fate inside the coffin that I had arranged for myself. I slowly turned the knob and quietly eased the door shut so as not to wake my sleeping family. I stood there in the dark for a moment or two, as if I were waiting to see if there was any ounce of hope left; if maybe I would change my mind about the decision that I had made, but nothing came.

I went over to my desk and pulled out a pair of hair cutting scissors that I kept in a drawer. I turned on the light to my closet and I eased my body down to the floor, aching and exhausted. I stared at the blade for what felt like hours, firmly pressing my finger into the sharp edge, feeling that old familiar pinch.

Once again, my family crossed my mind. I wondered if they would feel relief-like I would-that it was finally over. I tried to come up with just one reason not to do it, and I could not. I wasn't afraid anymore.

I began to cut into the soft underside of my arm, as I had done countless times before. Yet this time, there was no hesitation.

I was ready to die.

Something I have struggled to explain took place in that moment. As I was cutting my arm open to take my life, somehow, I fell asleep.

I awoke in a fog a couple of hours later, confused as to what had happened. Part of me briefly wondered if I was dead or not.

I looked down at the open wound on my arm and tried to recall exactly what had occurred and why it hadn't worked. I had never experienced anything like that before.

It was in that moment that I heard it-a clear thought in my head, so vivid amongst the stream of confusion:

"You're not getting off that easy.
I'm not done with you yet."

I can't tell you how I knew but somehow, somewhere deep inside of me, I knew that it was something greater than me, and it had saved me from myself.
I was furious.
I distinctly remember thinking, almost as if arguing with this unseen force of the universe,

"Why won't you let me die?"

I don't recall there being an answer to this question, but I do remember a subtle feeling of acceptance washing over me. A wave of calm and peace filled my heart.
I proceeded to pick myself up off the floor and I made my way into the bathroom to start wrapping my arm with gauze and bandages.

My brother, who was oblivious to what had just transpired, came downstairs a short while later as I sat on the couch watching tv; he asked me how I was feeling, if I had eaten anything, and he offered to make me some soup.
We talked for a while and I accepted the food he had offered me, and I wondered to myself how my family could still love and care for me after all that I had put them through. Their unconditional love was a force to be reckoned with, bending but never breaking despite all that I had done to them.

My dad came over the next day, and we all sat outside on the porch as he was telling us how they injected him with radioactive beads (to fight the cancer) and how he was supposed to stay away from small children and pregnant women for a couple of weeks.

He spoke about it casually, as if we weren't talking about his impending death. That was my dad though, if he was scared, he never showed it.

My senses felt heightened and every part of me felt raw. The withdrawals were winding down and my body was struggling to adjust to the world as it is-without the drugs.
Heroin tends to make everything dull and quiet.

You fade away and the color drains out of everything. It takes away the pain, but it takes away all the good, too. It robs you of joy, gratitude, beauty, peace. It turns you into this empty shell and life ceases to hold any sort of wonder or excitement.

On the day before I was set to go into rehab, I had come to the decision that I should get the boy's iPod back that I had stolen and pawned.
I wanted to start out this new chapter of my life on the right foot.
There was a part of me that expected him to praise me for my courage and for doing the right thing.
I don't know why I thought that's what would happen.

I sat on his couch while he stood above me, his eyes darkened with hurt and fury. I remained quiet, while he yelled, and I took it all in and I knew that I deserved it. For the iPod, for everything that I had ever done to treat him poorly when all he ever did was stand by my side. My betrayal cut the both of us deeply.

He scolded me for some time while I silently sobbed, staring at my hands that were folded neatly in my lap. Eventually he ran out of anger and all that was left in the room was silence and hurt. He asked me to get out of his apartment; he didn't want me there.
I stood before him, this man that I loved, tears falling down my face and my heart just broke. I wanted so badly to take it back.
He looked at me, and his heart broke for me, for the last time.
Sighing, he wrapped me in a hug,

"Get your shit together, Sarah."

My heart was in pieces. I felt like an empty shell, like my strength and my breath had been taken from me.
I walked out the door, wondering if I would ever see him again. I looked at this man, and I thought to myself that I would not be able to breathe without him.
Without him, the world would be void of air and sunlight.

I quickly walked out into the parking garage and got back into my mom's car, my face red and damp from sobbing.
There was no need for questions.
She looked at me with silent worry painted in her expression, wondering how this would affect my decision to get sober.

We stopped off at an old bar on the way home and went inside to get a drink.

I felt so raw, yet with the strangest feeling like my whole entire life was ahead of me, like it was only the beginning.
I couldn't explain where this feeling came from, it was just there, deep inside my chest.

My mom and I ordered two shots of rum, and, holding them in the air to make a toast, there was a pause as we both considered what we were toasting to. I wiped the last of the tears from my face, I raised my glass,

"To the last time."

She remained silent for a moment, peering at me with an expression of uncertainty,

"I hope so."

She looked exhausted, and I knew that I had put her, myself, and everyone in my life, through absolute hell for over a decade.
I was exhausted, too.

"It is- I can't tell you how I know, but I just know."

And I meant it.

CPSIA information can be obtained
at www.ICGtesting.com
Printed in the USA
LVHW021312031222
734485LV00013B/1127

9 781088 002261